CONTEMPORARY WRITERS

General Editors
MALCOLM BRADBURY
and
CHRISTOPHER BIGSBY

SEAMUS HEANEY

SEAMUS
HEANEY

BLAKE MORRISON

METHUEN
LONDON AND NEW YORK

First published in 1982 by
Methuen & Co. Ltd
11 New Fetter Lane, London EC4P 4EE
Published in the USA by
Methuen & Co.
in association with Methuen, Inc.
733 Third Avenue, New York, NY 10017

Typeset by Rowland Phototypesetting Ltd
Printed in Great Britain by
Richard Clay (The Chaucer Press) Ltd
Bungay, Suffolk

British Library Cataloguing in Publication Data

Morrison, Blake
Seamus Heaney. – (Contemporary writers)
1. Heaney, Seamus – Criticism and interpretation
I. Title   II. Series
821'.914   PR6058.E2
ISBN 0-416-31900-9

Library of Congress Cataloging in Publication Data

Morrison, Blake.
Seamus Heaney.
(Contemporary writers)
Bibliography: p.
1. Heaney, Seamus – Criticism and interpretation.
I. Title.   II. Series.
PR6058.E2Z78   821'.914   81-22586
ISBN 0-416-31900-9 (pbk.)   AACR2

CONTENTS

GENERAL EDITORS' PREFACE

Over the past twenty years or so, it has become clear that a decisive change has taken place in the spirit and character of contemporary writing. There now exists around us, in fiction, drama and poetry, a major achievement which belongs to our experience, our doubts and uncertainties, our ways of perceiving – an achievement stylistically radical and novel, and likely to be regarded as quite as exciting, important and innovative as that of any previous period. This is a consciousness and a confidence that has grown very slowly. In the 1950s it seemed that, somewhere amidst the dark realities of the Second World War, the great modernist impulse of the early years of this century had exhausted itself, and that the post-war arts would be arts of recessiveness, pale imitation, relative sterility. Some, indeed, doubted the ability of literature to survive the experiences of holocaust. A few major figures seemed to exist, but not a style or a direction. By the 1960s the confidence was greater, the sense of an avant-garde returned, the talents multiplied, and there was a growing hunger to define the appropriate styles, tendencies and forms of a new time. And by the 1970s it was not hard to see that we were now surrounded by a remarkable, plural, innovative generation, indeed several layers of generations, whose works represented radical inquiry into contemporary forms and required us to read and understand – or, often, to read and *not* understand –

in quite new ways. Today, as the 1980s start, that cumulative post-war achievement has acquired a degree of coherence that allows for critical response and understanding; hence the present series.

We thus start it in the conviction that the age of Beckett, Borges, Nabokov, Bellow, Pynchon, Robbe-Grillet, Golding, Murdoch, Fowles, Grass, Handke and Calvino, of Albee, Mamet, Shepard, Ionesco, Orton, Pinter and Stoppard, of Ginsberg, Lowell, Ashbery, Paz, Larkin and Hughes, and many another, is indeed an outstanding age of international creation, striking experiment, and some degree of aesthetic coherence. It is a time that has been described as 'post-modern', in the sense that it is an era consequent to modernism yet different from it, having its own distinctive preoccupations and stylistic choices. That term has its limitations, because it is apt to generate too precise definitions of the contemporary experiment, and has acquired rather too specific associations with contemporary American writing; but it does help concentrate our sense of living in a distinctive period. With the new writing has come a new criticism or rather a new critical theorem, its thrust being 'structuralist' or 'deconstructive' – a theorem that not only coexists with but has affected that writing (to the point where many of the best theorists write fictions, the best fictionalists write criticism). Again, its theory can be hermetic and enclosing, if not profoundly apocalyptic; but it points to the presence in our time of a new sense of the status of word and text, author and reader, which shapes and structures the making of modern form.

The aim of 'Contemporary Writers' is to consider some of the most important figures in this scene, looking from the standpoint of and at the achievement of the writers themselves. Its aims are eclectic, and it will follow no tight definition of the contemporary; it will function on the assumption that contemporary writing is by its nature multidirectional and elusive, since styles and directions keep constantly changing in writers who, unlike the writers of the past, are continuous, incomplete,

7

not dead (though several of these studies will address the careers of those who, though dead, remain our contemporaries, as many of those who continue to write are manifestly not). A fair criticism of living writers must be assertive but also provisional, just as a fair sense of contemporary style must be open to that most crucial of contemporary awarenesses, that of the suddenness of change. We do not assume, then, that there is one right path to contemporary experiment, nor that a self-conscious reflexiveness, a deconstructive strategy, an art of performance or a metafictional mode is the only one of current importance. As Iris Murdoch said, 'a strong agile realism which is of course not photographic naturalism' – associated perhaps especially with British writing, but also with Latin-American and American – is also a major component of modern style.

So in this series we wish to identify major writers, some of whom are avant-garde, others who are familiar, even popular, but all of whom are in some serious sense contemporary and in some contemporary sense serious. The aim is to offer brief, lucid studies of their work which draw on modern theoretical issues but respond, as much modern criticism does not, to their distinctiveness and individual interest. We have looked for contributors who are engaged with their subjects – some of them being significant practising authors themselves, writing out of creative experience, others of whom are critics whose interest is personal as well as theoretical. Each volume will provide a thorough account of the author's work so far, a solid bibliography, a personal judgement – and, we hope, an enlarged understanding of writers who are important, not only because of the individual force of their work, but because they are ours in ways no past writer could really be.

Norwich, England, 1981   MALCOLM BRADBURY
                                            CHRISTOPHER BIGSBY

ACKNOWLEDGEMENTS

Several people have helped my work on Heaney, either recently or in the past: I should like to thank Richard Brown, Patricia Craig, Steve Ellis, Edna Longley, Karl Miller, Andrew Motion, Tom Paulin, Craig Raine and John Silverlight; their assistance deserved a more substantial book than this one.

I should also like to thank the editors of the *New Statesman* and of the critical anthology *British Poetry Since 1970* (Manchester: Carcanet, 1980), in whose pages I first wrote about *Field Work* and *North*; both these pieces have been substantially rewritten and expanded here.

The author and publisher would like to thank the following for permission to reproduce copyright material: Faber & Faber Ltd for extracts from *Wintering Out*, *North*, *Door into the Dark* and *Death of a Naturalist* by Seamus Heaney; Faber & Faber Ltd and Farrar, Straus & Giroux, Inc. for extracts from *Field Work* and *Preoccupations: Selected Prose 1968–1978* by Seamus Heaney; Seamus Heaney and Ulsterman Publications for extracts from *Stations*.

A NOTE ON THE TEXTS

Page references to quotations from Seamus Heaney's works are taken from the British editions listed in the Bibliography.

The following abbreviations have been used:

DN *Death of a Naturalist*
DD *Door into the Dark*
WO *Wintering Out*
S *Stations*
N *North*
FW *Field Work*
P *Preoccupations: Selected Prose 1968–1978*

1

INTRODUCTION

Seamus Heaney is widely believed to be one of the finest poets now writing. To call him 'the most important Irish poet since Yeats' has indeed become something of a cliché. In Britain he is as essential a part of the school and university syllabus as are his post-1945 predecessors Philip Larkin and Ted Hughes; in America scholarly articles reflect a growing interest in his work; on both sides of the Atlantic influential critics – Christopher Ricks, Karl Miller, Clive James, Harold Bloom and Irvin Ehrenpreis among them – have pressed large claims on his behalf. He has won most of the literary prizes it is possible for a poet to win. His books enjoy large sales – *North*, for example, has sold over 30,000 copies and none of his collections less than 15,000. He is in constant demand for lecture tours, readings, interviews, and radio and television programmes. He seems to be that rare thing, a poet rated highly by critics and academics yet popular with 'the common reader'.

Unanimity of this kind is always likely to inspire suspicion. We expect genuinely innovative writers to cause us difficulty, to provoke shock and disagreement, to be assimilated only after a decent interval. Yet Heaney, it appears, is not a writer of this sort. Along with the acclaim, he has acquired the reputation of being a simple, straightforward, readily accessible writer whose methods and ideas owe more to the nineteenth century than the twentieth. A backwater all to himself, he is seen as lying outside the main currents of contemporary European and Anglo-American intellectual life; a throwback to an earlier age, he is admired precisely for not being a 'modern'.

Heaney himself, it must be admitted, has played no small part in the creation of this image. Relaxed and genial in manner, he likes to present himself as a sturdy, traditional craftsman whose eyes are firmly fixed on the past. Where contemporaries like Larkin, Hughes and Geoffrey Hill have been rather shy of passing comment on their work, Heaney, by contrast, has been an amenable and persuasive self-commentator who can be relied on to give useful and fascinating insights into his art: his reviews, interviews and lectures show him to be his own best critic. But he has also allowed, rather in the manner of Robert Frost and perhaps not wholly unintentionally, a considerably simplified version of his achievement to prevail both here and in America. His very willingness to talk about his work has delimited critical approaches to it.

The most serious drawback of taking Heaney on his own terms is that it means having to make vital concessions about the scale and importance of his work, perhaps even to accept that it is 'minor' poetry. Significantly, the one dissenter amid the general chorus of praise, A. Alvarez, has turned Heaney's self-image against him, using the word 'Victorian' about his poetry and claiming that it 'works comfortably in a recognizable tradition', 'challenges no presuppositions', 'does not advance into unknown territory'.[1] This, I fear, is the logical culmination of the established line on Heaney: he has a safe reputation but also a reputation for safety. We are encouraged to enjoy his work but not to see it as part of a world that includes Ashbery, Ammons, Pynchon, Grass, Stoppard, Fowles, Barthes, Derrida and Foucault. The bold contemporary spirit of those writers is, we are made to understand, quite alien to him.

One does not have to look very deeply into Heaney's work, however, to see that it is rather less comforting and comfortable than has been supposed. Far from being 'whole', it is tense, torn, divided against itself; far from being straightforward, it is layered with often obscure allusions; far from being archaic, it registers the tremors and turmoils of its age, forcing traditional forms to accept the challenge of harsh, intractable material. In short, Heaney's poetry has been seriously misrepresented, not least by its admirers. A proper response to Heaney's work requires reference to complex matters of ancestry, nationality, religion, history and politics, ones that a brief biographical account may help to outline.

Seamus Heaney was born in April 1939 in the townland of Mossbawn, County Derry, Northern Ireland, the eldest of nine children (the death in a road accident of one of his brothers is described in the poem 'Mid-Term Break'), and the son of a Catholic farmer and cattle dealer. The family was of solid farming stock, but it soon became clear that Seamus himself was likely to break with this tradition: after attending the local primary school in Anahorish (a 'mixed' school that took both Protestants and Catholics), he won scholarships first to St Columb's College, a Catholic boarding school in Londonderry (he was a boarder there from 1951 to 1957), and then to the Queen's University, Belfast, where he studied from 1957 to 1961, eventually taking a first-class honours degree in English language and literature. It was after graduation, when he was in his early twenties, that he began to publish poems in local university magazines and Belfast papers. Up until this point, he had, apparently, been more interested in pursuing his studies, had written little or no poetry, and had read next to nothing of contemporary verse. Now, as he worked as an English teacher in St Thomas's Secondary School, Belfast (1962–3), and at St Joseph's College (1963–6), he developed quickly, having poems accepted by the *New Statesman* in 1964 and by other prestigious London periodicals thereafter. The years 1965–6 were a turning-point for him in various ways: he married Marie Devlin and had the first of his three children; was appointed a lecturer in English at his old university, Queen's;

and had his first collection of poems published by Faber and Faber at the age of twenty-seven. Belfast continued to be his home – he lived there for fifteen years in all. But shortly after his return from a year as a guest lecturer at the University of California, Berkeley, in 1970–1, he resigned his teaching job at Queen's and moved to County Wicklow in the Republic of Ireland. In 1976 he settled in Dublin, where he works part-time at a Catholic college of education and lives in a house overlooking Dublin Bay.

As even so flimsy a sketch may suggest, Heaney's cultural identity is a complex one. He grew up in the North of Ireland, which technically at least makes him British; and it was in London, not in Dublin, that he was first published and taken up. But he is also a Northern Irish Catholic and part, therefore, of a minority that belongs officially to the United Kingdom but which has always looked to the south and the Republic. Heaney appears from an early age to have been very conscious of such ambiguities and divisions, inscribed as they were in local topography (his father's farm lay between a Protestant planter's estate and a town of local nationalist sentiment). They were present too in his childhood reading – Celtic legends, sectarian ballads and Catholic prayers on the one hand, *Alice in Wonderland*, Biggles and *Treasure Island* on the other. Later his affiliations became more complex still: aside from 'Irish' and 'English' (Yeats and Joyce but also Wordsworth and Hopkins), he became aware of the existence of a specifically Ulster literature that includes *The Tain*, Patrick Kavanagh, Louis MacNeice and John Montague as well as contemporaries like Michael Longley and Derek Mahon. We need to be aware of how participation in these different traditions brings out different elements in Heaney, ones that the term 'Anglo-Irish', with its associations of the Southern Protestant landed gentry, does not adequately cover.

Heaney's place in twentieth-century poetic tradition is also full of ambivalence and contradiction. Quaintly inhabiting a world in which Ezra Pound and 'making it new' might never have happened, he has embraced the role of Romantic poet, drawing his theories of composition from Wordsworth and comparing the poet's task to that of carpenters, water-diviners, blacksmiths, thatchers and a whole range of folksy-craftsy 'makers'. Yet his poetry has also been shaped by the modes of post-war Anglo-American poetry: it comes after the 1950s 'rationalism' of Larkin, Gunn, Davie, Wilbur, Roethke and Nemerov on the one hand, and the 1960s 'extremism' of Hughes, Plath, Redgrove, Lowell, Berryman and Sexton on the other, taking something from both camps while going forward into a new domain. Moreover, Heaney's preoccupation with language and with questions of authorial control makes him part of a still larger modern intellectual movement which has emphasized that language is not a transparent medium by means of which a writer says what he intends to, but rather something self-generating, infinitely productive, exceeding us as individuals. Heaney's belief that the poet does not so much master language as surrender to it might look like a Romantic theory of 'inspiration', but it also bears surprising resemblances to recent structuralist discourse, some of which he is certainly acquainted with.[2] There is the shared notion of language working through the medium of the author rather than the author through language.

A final example of Heaney's ambivalence concerns his response to the recent history of Northern Ireland, the crisis of which has placed poets under the compulsion to 'respond'. Heaney has written poems directly about the Troubles as well as elegies for friends and acquaintances who have died in them; he has tried to discover a historical framework in which to interpret the current unrest; and he has taken on the mantle of public spokesman, someone looked to for comment and guidance. Yet he has also shown signs of deeply resenting this role, defending the right of poets to be private and apolitical, and questioning the extent to which poetry, however 'committed', can influence the course of history. His own ambivalence has been reflected by that of his critics: some have praised him for

15

remaining outside the political arena, others have applauded his participation; some have accused him of not siding sufficiently with Northern Catholic Republican aspirations, others have complained that he has not come out decisively enough against the IRA. There are, in short, important questions to be asked about Heaney's role as a historical witness. His response to those who have urged him to declare his beliefs has been to say simply 'Read the poems': this is not mere evasiveness, for as we shall see Heaney's poetry has quite unmistakable leanings and loyalties, and it is there, as he implies, that we should begin.

2

THE GAG OF PLACE:
'DEATH OF A NATURALIST' AND
'DOOR INTO THE DARK'

The Catholics in the North aren't the 'typical Irish'. Some
noble wild-eyed figure with a great flow of eloquence and
wit, with a kind of primitive energy about him, untrammelled in some way. My people were not like that at all. They
were quiet, watchful, oblique, sly.[3]

The most striking feature of Seamus Heaney's first two books,
his work of the sixties, is not their sensuousness of language,
nor their tough physicality, nor their celebration of Irish
customs and crafts, nor even their description of rural life; it is
their mediation between silence and speech. One would hardly
think so, to judge from conventional accounts of his early
poetry. *Death of a Naturalist* (1966) and *Door into the Dark*
(1969) were received at the time of publication, and have
been thought about ever since, as examples of post-1945
nature poetry – an imprecisely defined genre, but one presided
over by Ted Hughes and reputed to be in opposition to
'idealized' Georgian treatments of nature because of its emphasis on the harsh, actual, predatory and corruptible. Early
reviews of Heaney speedily assimilated him into this genre:
there was talk of his 'fidelity to his rural experience',[4] of his
poetry's being 'loud with the slap of the spade and sour with the
stink of turned earth',[5] and of how 'his words give us the
soil-reek of Ireland, the colourful violence of his childhood on a
farm in Derry'.[6] Such reviews set the terms for subsequent
critical discussion of Heaney's work. It is as a twin to the
early Ted Hughes, as a fellow demolisher of the *Golden*

Treasury treatment of nature, that he has found his way into the school and university syllabus.

It would be perverse to pretend that there is not some justice in this view of Heaney's work. Ted Hughes's influence indeed permeates many of the early poems about farming and country matters, and spills over into Heaney's use of assonance, metaphor, and titles as opening words of the poem. 'Turkeys Observed', for example ('One observes them, one expects them; / Blue-breasted in their indifferent mortuary'; *DN*, p. 37), is very like poems in Hughes's *Lupercal* (1960), and we have Heaney's own testimony that when he first read this book in his early twenties it made a deep impression on him:

> I remember the day I opened Ted Hughes's *Lupercal* in the Belfast Public Library. [There was] a poem called 'View of a Pig' and in my childhood we'd killed pigs on the farm, and I'd seen pigs shaved, hung up, and so on. . . . Suddenly, the matter of contemporary poetry was the material of my own life. I had had some notion that modern poetry was far beyond the likes of me – there was Eliot and so on – so I got this thrill out of trusting my own background, and I started a year later, I think.[7]

We also know that when he was studying and teaching in Belfast in the early 1960s Heaney received the tuition of Philip Hobsbaum, a contemporary of Ted Hughes at Cambridge, and a fervent believer in his work; Hobsbaum encouraged Heaney to strive for Hughes's muscularity and energy.

Yet, if we insist on reading Heaney's first two books purely in these terms, we are obliged to call them at best apprentice work and at worst clumsy and derivative. What passed once for freshness, spontaneity and 'innocence' would now look like a fatal tendency to fall back on the example of others in the most gauche possible way. For, as well as sounding like a hobnailed version of Hughes, Heaney is also awkwardly imitative of a good number of other modern British poets. Examples of this gaucheness are not hard to discover. There is the absurd circumlocution in 'An Advancement of Learning' (a version of D. H. Lawrence's 'Snake', despite its Baconian title) which makes Heaney refer to a rat he has previously avoided facing as 'my hitherto snubbed rodent'; or the ham-fisted introduction in 'The Play Way' (a rewrite of Yeats's 'Among School Children') of the Eliotic 'Mixing memory and desire with chalk dust'; or the overkill of 'Trout' (from the same finny school of poetry as Hughes's 'Pike'), which asks us, within seventeen short lines, to imagine the fish as a gun-barrel, torpedo, dart, tracer-bullet, ramrod and volley; or the clanking final couplet of 'Scaffolding' (a poetic conceit that might have come from the Movement anthology *New Lines* (1955)), which patly affirms a love-relationship: 'We may let the scaffolds fall / Confident that we have built our wall' (*DN*, p. 50). Throughout these first two books Heaney looks distinctly unhappy in his use of iambic pentameters and quatrains, repeatedly wrenching his rhythms and rhymes. To compare his work with the work it borrows from is a damaging exercise.

But there are other ways to approach his early poetry, ways that lead us from what is immature and debilitating and point towards his central strengths. What anyone reading Heaney's early work for the first time today would immediately be struck by is the tendency they share with certain works of the modern spirit (not least Beckett's plays) to weigh inarticulacy against articulation, to acknowledge the claims of silence as well as those of speech. And what such a reader would secondly be struck by is that, like certain writers who have earned the tag 'post-modernist' (Borges and Ashbery, for example), Heaney devotes much of his energy to producing a literature that is about itself. His first book begins with an image of him holding a pen (in 'Digging') and ends with him gazing like some 'big-eyed Narcissus' into a well: 'I rhyme / To see myself, to set the darkness echoing' he tells us ('Personal Helicon'); and such narcissistic self-consciousness about the business of writing is indeed a major theme of his work. In this company of minimalists, absurdists and termination theorists, Heaney cuts an unlikely figure, and it must be said that he comes at the themes of silence and solipsism from his own special angle. None the less it is impossible now to read *Death of a Naturalist* and *Door into the Dark* without noticing these two preoccupations.

The preoccupations arise from the same source: Heaney's sense of belonging to a silent ancestry, an ancestry with which he, as someone who went away to boarding school on a scholarship at the age of eleven (he was an early beneficiary of the 1947 Education Act, which gave Northern Catholics greater educational opportunities) and who has become a writer, has embarrassed relations. What links the various traders, labourers and craftsmen who fill his first two books is that, unlike him, they are lacking in speech. His water-diviner works 'without a word'. His Lough Neagh fishermen, whether out in a boat or eel-catching in the fields, carefully avoid noise ('better not clatter now'), allowing themselves only terse epigrams and prophecies – 'We'll be the quicker going down', 'The lough will claim a victim every year', 'Once the season's in'. The haymakers in 'A Wife's Tale' are seen 'smoking and saying nothing'. On a 'Dawn Shoot' the narrator and his companion remain 'mostly silent'. A thatcher, though 'bespoke for weeks' (a nice word-play in the context), goes wordlessly about his business, leaving his clients 'gaping'. The blacksmith, returning to his forge from the half-door he has been leaning on, merely 'grunts'. A docker sits 'strong and blunt as a Celtic cross, / Clearly used to silence' (*DN*, p. 41): he demands 'quiet' of his family and practises tight-lipped extremity himself – 'Speech is clamped in the lips' vice.' That final image is one that might stand as an epigraph for Heaney's early work, and its obsession with silence.

In this culture of clamped speech, 'curt' is the most popular adjective and 'curtly' the most popular adverb. The adjective turns up in 'The Outlaw', for example, where the poem's speaker brings a cow to be serviced by the 'unlicensed bull' kept by Old Kelly:

He grunted a curt 'Go by

> Get up on that gate'. And from my lofty station
> I watched the business-like conception.
>
> The door, unbolted, whacked back against the wall.
> The illegal sire fumbled from his stall
>
> Unhurried as an old steam engine shunting.
> He circled, snored and nosed. No hectic panting,
>
> Just the unfussy ease of a good tradesman . . . (*DD*, p. 16)

Old Kelly is typical of Heaney's protagonists in managing to make little more than a half-utterance from the back of the throat. Yelps, grunts, gulps, snores, whoops, coughs – these are the common sounds. Kelly and his kind are identified with their animals, which also lack the power of conversation. Their animals, in turn, are identified with them: Kelly's bull has 'the unfussy ease of a good tradesman' and thus resembles not only Kelly but the water-diviner, who is 'professionally unfussed'. Taciturnity is a mark of proficiency: getting the job done means eschewing the luxury of words. Not surprisingly, then, speech marks are one kind of punctuation almost entirely absent from these two books: there are sixty-odd poems but, aside from the homilies of the Lough Neagh fisherman, Kelly's curt request to 'Get up on that gate', and the loquacious 'Wife's Tale', we have only five examples of direct speech, none of them amounting to more than a line or so.

Silence is golden, paucity of speech a plus. Noise, on the other hand, becomes a threat. It is the rat which 'slobbered', 'smudging the silence'; or the terrifying 'slabber' of a waterfall, 'like villains dropped screaming to justice'; or the 'tragic chorus in a gale'. The title poem of Heaney's first book uses noise to denote loss of innocence. In the first part of the poem the child at its centre is cocooned in a warm, womb-like world of tadpoles and frogspawn; in the second part the waters are broken by the arrival of 'angry frogs' invading the flax-dam:

> I ducked through hedges

21

To a coarse croaking that I had not heard
Before. The air was thick with a bass chorus.
Right down the dam gross-bellied frogs were cocked
On sods; their loose necks pulsed like sails. Some hopped:
The slap and plop were obscene threats. Some sat
Poised like mud grenades, their blunt heads farting.
I sickened, turned, and ran. The great slime kings
Were gathered for vengeance and I knew
That if I dipped my hand the spawn would clutch it.

(DN, pp. 15–16)

The child's experience has affinities with the 'act of stealth' described in Book I of Wordsworth's *The Prelude*: as the boy Wordsworth receives nature's retribution for his taking of the boat, so the boy Heaney connects his earlier taking of frog-spawn with this noisy 'vengeance' of the adult frogs. What is noticeable about the Heaney poem is that terror should be evoked not through eerie nighttime silence (as it is in Wordsworth and in the other forerunner to this poem, Hughes's 'Pike') but through a violent 'bass chorus' and assonantal nightmare – 'cocked', 'sods', 'plop', 'obscene'. The poem may be laboured (its pentameters either too condensed or too strung out), but it leaves us in no doubt of the trauma of the child's experience.

Music and song might be thought to offer a means to release noise in a more structured and acceptable way, but Heaney seems not at all convinced of this. In 'The Folk Singers', an unusual poem for him because of its almost bitter, satirical note, he attacks the singers for their 'slick' performance of 'time-turned words': 'Death's edge / Blunts on the narcotic strumming.' Like Yeats in 'The Scholars', he sees the vulnerable expression of young lovers – 'Lines / That young men, tossing on their beds, / Rhymed out in love's despair' (Yeats), 'Numb passion, pearled in the shy / Shell of a country love' (Heaney; *DN*, p. 55) – being cheapened by second-hand interpreters, who despoil the ground-note of authentic feeling.

The poem is slight, even sentimental, but its defence of shyness is in keeping with the author's belief that the more modest and muted expression is, the nearer to silence, the better. The idea recurs in 'Twice Shy', a title that tells us both that the couple in the poem have been 'bitten' by love and that they are two naturally shy people. Shyness is again to be taken as a sign of integrity: we know that this is an intense relationship ('still waters running deep') because of the lovers' 'nervous childish talk', their 'chary' manner with each other, their reluctance 'to publish feeling'. If they are immature, this is to their credit: throughout *Death of a Naturalist* Heaney equates maturity (whether in blackberries, frogs or people) with corruption.

The cumulative effect of these poems is to suggest that as a young poet Seamus Heaney found himself in the position of valuing silence above speech, of defending the shy and awkward against the confident and accomplished, of feeling language to be a kind of betrayal. This might be thought a somewhat paradoxical position for a poet to take up. But the community Heaney came from, and with which he wanted his poetry to express solidarity, was one on which the pressure of silence weighed heavily. It was not only rural, renowned like all rural communities for its inwardness and reserve, but also Northern Irish and Catholic, with additional reasons for clamming up. 'Whatever you say, say nothing' was a piece of wisdom Heaney heard from his mother, and later became the title of a sequence of poems in which he describes 'The famous / Northern reticence, the tight gag of place / And times', explaining its origins:

Smoke-signals are loud-mouthed compared with us:
Manoeuvrings to find out name and school,
Subtle discrimination by addresses
With hardly an exception to the rule

That Norman, Ken and Sidney signalled Prod
And Seamus (call me Sean) was sure-fire Pape.

O land of password, handgrip, wink and nod,
Of open minds as open as a trap,

Where tongues lie coiled, as under flames lie wicks,
Where half of us, as in a wooden horse
Were cabin'd and confined like wily Greeks,
Besieged within the siege, whispering morse. (N, pp. 59–60)

Heaney here supplies some of the political and religious factors that lay behind the silence of his people. He grew up in a culture of the 'siege mentality', where Catholics were always suspected (often justifiably) of harbouring IRA arms and activists, such suspicions being particularly strong during the Second World War and again in the late 1950s. Heaney was himself stopped when a teenager by the Royal Ulster Constabulary, as he relates in 'The Ministry of Fear', and had from his own brother an outstanding example of the 'gag of place and times': he relates in an interview how his brother was beaten up at a police station after having attended a Republican meeting, but how he didn't tell Heaney that this had happened to him until ten years later.[8]

Heaney's early poems do not analyse the reasons for his people's silence; they merely document it. But there is no doubt that this ancestry watermarked his psyche, creating inhibitions in him about the writing of poetry. When his work first began to appear in university magazines, he preferred not to put his name to it, adopting the pseudonym 'Incertus'. And even as he shed some of that uncertainty he continued to worry that to express himself freely, through literature, was in effect to betray the values of the tribe. The matter is touched on in an interview with John Haffenden:

Dan Jacobson said to me once, 'You feel bloody well guilty about writing', and there is indeed some part of me that is entirely unimpressed by the activity, that doesn't dislike it, but it's the generations, I suppose, of rural ancestors – not illiterate, but not literary. They, in me, or I, through them,

24

don't give a damn. I don't know whether that's a good thing or a bad thing.[9]

How, having been educated out of them, to keep faith with one's family and tribe? How to write a poetry that will honour that sense of 'not giving a damn' without wholly acceding to it? These questions, which have nagged at Heaney throughout his career, lie behind three early poems about his father, 'Digging', 'Follower' and 'Boy Driving His Father to Confession', all of which are anxious to assert an intimacy between father and son. In the last of these, an uncollected poem written in 1965, he rehearses the four occasions in his life when his father has seemed close to him, the first on the death of one of Heaney's brothers (an experience treated at greater length in 'Mid-Term Break') and the last now, on the way to confession. The 'common ground' they discover seems smaller, however, than the distance between them:

> Here at the churchyard I am slowing down
> To meet you, the fourth time, on common ground.
> You grunt, and slam the door. I watch another
> Who gropes as awkwardly to know his father.[10]

The relationship explored in this poem – the grunting, impenetrable father with his 'thick grey skull', the earnestly probing son who wants to fathom and get close to him – is reproduced in slightly different form in 'Follower'. Here the father is seen at work, ploughing, silent and remote (the only sound he makes is his 'clicking tongue'), while the 'yapping' son desperately follows him about. The adult's skill at 'mapping the furrow exactly' is contrasted with the clumsiness of the child, only for this order of things to be reversed at the end:

> I wanted to grow up and plough,
> To close one eye, stiffen my arm.
> All I ever did was follow
> In his broad shadow round the farm.

I was a nuisance, tripping, falling,
Yapping always. But today
It is my father who keeps stumbling
Behind me, and will not go away. (*DN*, pp. 24–5)

The poem brings visually alive the figure of speech about a son
'following in his father's footsteps', and its reversal at the end
carries a possible double meaning: we can take it, literally, that
the father is now old and clinging; or, metaphorically, that the
son, as a writer, is shackled with his father as poetic subject-
matter. Whichever the reading, though, we are again struck
more by distance than by intimacy: not only do father and son
have different skills, but they are at the height of their powers at
different times. The common ground is divided ground.

The dilemma of following is not fully resolved in 'Digging',
either, but comes closer to being. This is the best-known and
most widely anthologized of all Heaney's poems, though he
himself has called it 'a big coarse-grained navvy of a poem' (*P*,
p. 43), and has conceded that 'a couple of lines in it . . . have
more of the theatricality of the gunslinger than the self-
absorption of the digger' (*P*, p. 41). There is indeed something
clumpingly deliberate about the way Heaney claims kinship
with his father by turning his writing implement into a violent
weapon: 'Between my finger and my thumb / The squat pen
rests; snug as a gun' (*DN*, p. 13). It is too macho, melodramati-
cally so, and not even the insertion of the adjectives 'squat' and
'snug' can allay the feeling that the analogy is in any case not
right – inaccurate visually and misleading in its implication
that what follows in *Death of a Naturalist* is the work of a
poetic hard man. The real interest of the image is that it seems
to be over-compensating for the poet's shame at departing
from lineage. The Heaneys had been associated with County
Derry since Gaelic times, and the poet is only too aware of the
fathers standing behind his father: 'By God, the old man could
handle a spade. / Just like his old man' (*DN*, p. 13). Heaney has
spoken of the gibes he used to hear as a boy – 'the pen's lighter

than the spade', 'learning's easy carried', 'Boys but this Seamus fellow is a great scholar. What book are you in now son?' (*P*, pp. 21 and 42) – and he seeks to answer them here by presenting his poetry as a form of agriculture. His own digging implement is voluble, not 'curt' like his father's, but it performs many of the same functions, passing on tradition, extracting 'new' produce (poems, not potatoes) out of old furrows, and enjoying an intimacy with the earth. Heaney's assertion at the end – 'I'll dig with it' – has not quite the conviction he intends, but it is the best case he can mount in his first two books.

These are not, then, poems of simple fidelity to the Derry countryside but poems anxious whether such fidelity is possible and, if so, what it costs. Far from enjoying some untroubled closeness to his home ground, Heaney feels torn between his roots and his reading, between 'words of the heart and hearth-language and the learned, public, socially acceptable language of school and salon'.[11] These diametrically opposed languages make up the texture of 'The Early Purges', a poem about the drowning of kittens which might easily be dismissed as another contribution to the violent, Hughesian nature school. It was seen as such when it was set as an O-level text in 1976, and caused some controversy.[12] But its real interest lies in the accommodation of three contrasting voices: the child who is upset by the drowning; the adult (Dan Taggart) who sees it as necessary; and the poet (a child now become an adult) who settles the matter in Dan Taggart's favour. The language of the poem embodies the different viewpoints: 'frail', 'soft', 'sadly', 'bobbed' – this is the voice of childhood feeling; 'soused', 'slung', 'snout', 'pump' – this is the curt Taggart; the third voice is the most sophisticated, since it acknowledges grown-up liberal attitudes that might sanction the child's untutored ones but then rejects them in favour of the voice of the tribe:

> Still, living displaces false sentiments
> And now, when shrill pups are prodded to drown
> I just shrug, 'Bloody pups'. It makes sense:

27

'Prevention of cruelty' talk cuts ice in town
Where they consider death unnatural,
But on well-run farms pests have to be kept down.

                                                              (*DN*, p. 23)

There is something deliberately tight-lipped, square-shouldered, even callous, about this poem – which may explain why he chose not to include it in his *Selected Poems*, when he assembled that volume from his first four books in 1980. It is one of several poems in which he takes pains to inform us that he lacks feeling, or at least finer feeling. Its interest is that this brutality again arises from an anxiety to 'keep faith': Heaney invokes the voices of his education only to send them packing.

*

In later work Heaney is better able to resolve this tension between roots and reading. In 'Singing School', for example, he self-consciously casts himself as a Stephen Duck figure – 'Those hobnailed boots from beyond the mountain / Were walking, by God, all over the fine / Lawns of elocution' (*N*, p. 64). But his early work finds it hard to empty these pockets of shame: blushingly torn between the lived and the learned, it is embarrassing for both poet and reader. What comfort and resolution Heaney found owe much to the example of the Irish poet Patrick Kavanagh, whose poetry he discovered in the early 1960s and for which he developed an increasing respect throughout the decade. Having lived in both County Monaghan and Dublin, Kavanagh seemed to Heaney to illustrate the same split he himself was experiencing between 'the illiterate self that was tied to the little hills and earthed in the stony grey soil, and the literate self that pined for "the city of Kings / Where art, music and letters were the real things"' (*P*, p. 137). Kavanagh's volume *The Great Hunger* (1942) impressed Heaney because of its unsentimental, undramatic presentation of the daily agricultural round, its 'intimacy with actual clay and a desperate sense that life in the secluded spot is no book of pastoral hours but an enervating round of labour and lethargy' (*P*, p. 122). It also seemed to him, as his essays on Kavanagh

28

make clear, to be informed by 'the penalty of consciousness, the unease generated when a milieu becomes material' (*P*, p. 118): it was the kind of rural poetry that only someone who had been exposed to broader horizons could have written. If Kavanagh had not existed, Heaney would have had to invent him: he needed the example of an Irish poet through whom he could place himself – and Yeats would not serve. And if in a sense he *did* invent Kavanagh, finding 'love and celebration' in *The Great Hunger* that are not really there but which, if they were, would sanction his own reverential tone, he did appropriate him to a useful end. Kavanagh's assurance that 'Parochialism is universal; it deals with fundamentals' made Heaney less squirmingly self-conscious about drawing on his rural upbringing.

There was also the encouragement gained from being part of a poetic community in Belfast. The weekly seminars initiated by Philip Hobsbaum, who had arrived at the Queen's University to teach English in 1960, brought Heaney into contact with Michael Longley, Derek Mahon, James Simmons and other aspiring poets. Heaney himself has described the importance of these meetings:

> When Hobsbaum arrived in Belfast he moved disparate elements into a single action. He emanated energy, generosity, belief in the community, trust in the parochial, the inept, the unprinted. He was impatient, dogmatic, relentlessly literary: yet he was patient with those he trusted, unpredictably susceptible to a wide variety of poems and personalities and urgent that the social and political exacerbations of our place should disrupt the decorums of literature. . . .
>
> What Hobsbaum achieved, whether people like it or not, was to give a generation a sense of themselves . . .
>
> (*P*, pp.28–9)

Heaney overstates Hobsbaum's catholicity of taste: it is clear that he favoured a poetry that combined the wit and metrical tightness of the Movement with the power and physicality of

29

Ted Hughes, a combination his young Derry protégé achieved only too well. But if Hobsbaum held Heaney back as well as helping him forward, he did at least enable him to meet Longley and Mahon, who had returned north after studying together at Trinity College, Dublin. The three soon became close friends, dedicating poems to each other and later exchanging verse-letters – 'the tight-assed trio' Michael Foley dubbed them.[13] Though both published their first collections after Heaney (Mahon his *Night-Crossing* in 1968, Longley his *No Continuing City* in 1969), they were in some respects more sophisticated and cosmopolitan than he was. Mahon's book, for example, shows considerable knowledge of European and modernist culture (Beckett, Dowson, De Quincey and Villon are among those alluded to), while Longley makes extensive use of classical myth. Friendship with Mahon and Longley matured Heaney and encouraged him to think, as Patrick Kavanagh did, that Northern Irish 'parochialism' might attain a kind of universality.

The story of the Belfast 'Group' is well known. Less recognized is that the 'Group' was part of a larger movement among Northern Irish intellectuals in the 1960s towards the rehabilitation of Ulster's cultural traditions. This was not quite the Irish Literary Revival of Yeats and Lady Gregory, but there was certainly a renewed interest in the preservation and definition of a disappearing culture. Several commissions were formed and White Papers produced which looked into the speaking, teaching and broadcasting of the Irish language, and work began on the still uncompleted *Ulster Dialect Dictionary*. Sean O'Riada (to whom Heaney later wrote an elegy) and others brought about a revival in traditional Irish music, one strengthened by the annual *Fleadh* music festivals. Historians such as J. C. Beckett, A. T. Q. Stewart and F. S. L. Lyons were at work on important research. The Ulster Folk Museum, initiated in 1958, was officially opened in 1964. The Belfast Festival of 1965 was a large-scale effort covered by the London press. Most important of all, perhaps, was the rural anthropology undertaken by E. Estyn Evans (then Professor of Geography and Director of the Institute of Irish Studies at Queen's) in his popular and still marvellously readable *Irish Folk Ways* (1957), a book that documented the actual material of traditional peasant life – spades, ploughs, kilns, looms, carts, boats, and so on – and which carried the warning that 'knowledge of ways of life that have altered little for centuries is passing away'.[14]

This general spirit of reverence towards the past helped Heaney resolve some of his awkwardness about being a writer: he could serve his own community by preserving in literature its customs and crafts, yet simultaneously gain access to a larger community of letters. In this the example of Estyn Evans was of special importance: *Irish Folk Ways* has descriptions of thatching (pp. 50–8), churning (pp. 95–8), cattle-dealing (pp. 259–60), ploughing (pp. 129–31) and forging (pp. 199–200) which Heaney was able to draw on for his own poems on these subjects. Sometimes the phrasing and ideas are very similar: on cattle-dealing at fairs, for instance, Evans speaks of 'the vigorous hand-slapping by which bargains are sealed in tight-lipped silence'; Heaney in 'Ancestral Photograph' sees his uncle 'Draw thumbs out of his waistcoat, curtly smack / Hands and sell' (*DN*, p. 27).[15]

But Heaney's strong, silent tradesmen are more than Estyn Evans look-alikes and more than the denizens of a dying culture. In their almost mystical oneness with the natural world, they are intended to stand as models for the poet: as he celebrates them, so they in turn guide and sanction his craft. The blacksmith has a 'door into the dark' and his anvil stands 'in the centre'. The salmon fisher likewise stands 'in the centre' of the stream, 'casting' into the unknown. The thatcher, laborious at the outset of his task ('It seemed he spent the morning warming up'), reveals a 'Midas touch' at the end. Churning is presented as a similarly alchemical process, transforming buttermilk into 'coagulated sunlight'. Most important of all, perhaps, is the water-diviner, silent himself but opening the channels of communication – 'Spring water suddenly broad-casting / Through a green aerial its secret stations' (*DN*, p. 36). All these craftsmen are pantheistic go-betweens, establishing bridges between the known and unknown.

Inspired by their example, Heaney promises in several poems from *Death of a Naturalist* and *Door into the Dark* to throw off the gag of place. Images of fluency, of water being released, are a feature of both books, but more especially of the second. These images have strong sexual overtones, suggesting the release of orgasm; and they have their origin in Celtic myth, which reveres springs and wells. But it is as a metaphor for a writer 'finding his voice' and overcoming the various blocks that afflict him that these images have most pertinence. 'Rite of Spring' is the nearest to being explicit about this, describing a frozen water-pump with 'a lump / In its throat' being warmed and unjammed. The first quatrain of 'Cana Revisited' has 'water locked behind the taps' and 'No expectation of miracu-lous words', but in the second quatrain the miracle or 'con-secration' is about to take place. 'Undine' is spoken in the voice of a stream given 'right of way' by a labourer. 'Frogman', an uncollected poem from 1968, follows the career of a diver whose work began as 'a job' and no more but who has now 'slipped away' into a new sphere of freedom and enjoyment – 'It's come to be / He just loves the water'.[16] In 'Bann Clay', the penultimate poem in *Door into the Dark*, the poet recalls cleaning a drain 'Till the water gradually ran / Clear on its old floor': it is the same liberation he seeks today as a poet – 'I labour / Towards it still'. Most exultant of all these poems about release is 'Saint Francis and the Birds', where the birds are 'like a flock of words / Released for fun' and where 'images [take] flight' – Francis is seen as a poet discovering his creative powers.

The fact that these images are more recurrent in *Door into the Dark* than in *Death of a Naturalist* reflects Heaney's growing confidence in his poetic abilities. Composition is no longer self-conscious labour but a matter of trust and trance:

'The Given Note', for example, eliminates the problem of how to write by suggesting that poetry is a 'spirit music' that comes naturally as if 'from nowhere' – 'He got this air out of the night'. Night and darkness also become important: in several poems we see Heaney resolving to go into them, poetry becoming a nocturnal and somnambulistic encounter. In *Death of a Naturalist* he had shunned such an exercise, deterred (as he records in 'The Barn') by his childhood Pascalian terror of the infinite spaces:

> The dark gulfed like a roof-space. I was chaff
> To be pecked up when the birds shot through the air-slits.
> I lay face-down to shun the fear above. (*DN*, p. 17)

But *Door into the Dark* is a less fearful collection, one more willing to acknowledge the fascination of darkness. Beginning, not wholly successfully, with three poems of dream and nightmare, it proceeds to make tentative probes into the unconscious, the secret sources of power, the old ancestral places. Variations round the word 'dark' – 'resumed the dark', 'a core of old dark', 'the darkened sphere', 'dark delivers him', 'the weltering dark' – are carried out with a thrill of pleasure, and the book ends by 'striking / Inwards and downwards' into the Jungian ground of the peat-bog, with its buried record of previous generations of Irish life.

Door into the Dark is more promise than fulfilment, more a hovering on the threshold than a decisive arrival. And purely in terms of the number of good poems it contains it can scarcely be called an advance on its predecessor: 'Bogland' and 'At Ardboe Point', for example, are extremely subtle and delicate poems, but over all there is not the weight to the collection that *Death of a Naturalist* attains through 'Digging', 'Follower', 'Churning Day' and 'Personal Helicon'. Indeed, what one remembers from both collections are not complete poems but isolated images of accurate visual perception: the 'little corrugated butter-spades' in 'Churning Day'; the potatoes in 'At a Potato Digging' which 'Split / by the spade . . . show white as cream'; the 'wet grass bleach[ing] our boots' in 'Blackberry-Picking'; the 'sweaty twist of the bellyband' and 'Green froth that lathered each end / Of the shining bit' in the equine 'Gone'; the 'unpredictable fantail of sparks / Or hiss when a new shoe toughens in water' in 'The Forge'; the combine in 'Night Drive' which 'bled seeds across its work-light'; above all, perhaps, the mosquitoes in 'At Ardboe Point' with their 'hail of fine chaff' and 'innocent shuttling choirs'. Nevertheless one ends the second book convinced that Heaney has begun to overcome the problems that plague the early part of his career. Having been preoccupied with 'finding himself', with placing himself in relation to both family and literary traditions, Heaney recognizes that a deeper and darker plunge is necessary. Renunciation of personal identity appeals to him as a way of opening up new dimensions of inquiry: 'You had to come back / To know how to lose yourself', as he puts it in 'The Plantation'. From 1969 on Heaney would still be coming back, to his home ground and tribe, but without the 'penalty of consciousness', and as if seeing them for the first time.

3

THE GUTTURAL MUSE:
'WINTERING OUT' AND 'STATIONS'

> The war in Ulster is being fought out on a narrower ground than even the most impatient observer might imagine, a ground every inch of which has its own associations and special meaning.
>
> The Ulsterman carries the map of this religious geography in his mind almost from birth. He knows which villages, which roads and streets, are Catholic, or Protestant, or 'mixed'. It not only tells him where he can, or cannot, wave an Irish tricolour or wear his Orange sash, but imposes on him a complex behaviour pattern and a special way of looking at political problems. The nuance is all-important. . . . To understand the full significance of any episode of sectarian conflict, you need to know the precise relationship of the locality in which it occurred to the rest of the mosaic of settlement. But the chequerboard on which the game is played has a third dimension. What happens in each square derives a part of its significance, and perhaps all of it, from what happened there at some time in the past. Locality and history are welded together.[17]

In June 1970 Ian Hamilton's poetry magazine *The Review* carried a feature called 'Where Are They Now?' in which four contemporary writers were caricatured as threatened species of animals. Seamus Heaney was one of these writers, appearing as a 'Longhorn Cow, a big, heavy and ungainly stock once widely distributed in England and Ireland.' The feature suggested that the 'fickle world of fashion' had once briefly flirted with Heaney, but had now thrown him over: '"Once I was a trout-tickling gypsy lad", murmured 48-year-old Seamus Heaney ruefully, "and now I am Ewart Milne, to be sure."'[18] Heaney was in fact a mere thirty-one when this satire appeared, with only two books behind him. But the parody indicates the stereotype in which he had begun to be cast. A year earlier Christopher Ricks had warned that Heaney would 'have to reconcile himself to the fact that *Door into the Dark* will consolidate him as the poet of muddy-booted blackberry-picking',[19] and, despite hints in that collection of possible advances, the English public had indeed firmly labelled him as a rustic, word-spinning Celt with an affection for the simple things of the countryside.

This was not, historically, very surprising. Terence Brown has shown in his study *Northern Voices* that there is a long tradition of Irish poets who have been taken up by the English, and then dropped, in this way. Ulster in the 1880s and 1890s provided a good number of them, including Alice Milligan, Ethna Carbery, James Cousins, Joseph Campbell and Richard Rowley, the last of whom had versions of pastoral such as the following:

> I've got a farm, an' a score o' sheep,
> An' a barn that the brown hens lays in,
> A fine thatched house, an' a mountain-side,
> Wi' forty acres o' grazin'.[20]

The dangers of this Anglo-Irish arrangement were apparent to Bernard Shaw in his day – he wrote in the preface to *Man and Superman* that 'The Englishman instinctively flatters the fault that makes the Irishman harmless and amusing to him' – and to Patrick Kavanagh in his: 'the English love "Irishmen" and are always on the look-out for them'.[21] At the end of the 1960s this seems to have become apparent to Heaney too: certainly his remark in a review of 1969 that contemporary Irish writers 'have grown wary of the PQ, i.e., peasant quality'[22] suggests an awareness of the perils of being patronized. So, too, the poems 'Servant Boy' and 'Bye-Child' from this period seem intended as sly declarations of resistance: in the first the 'Old work-whore, slave- / blood' who 'comes first-footing / the back doors of the little / barons' is quietly 'resentful / and impenitent' (*WO*, p. 17); in the second the 'henhouse boy', formerly confined to darkness and incapable of speech, learns to 'speak at last / With a remote mime / Of something beyond patience' (*WO*, p. 72). Looking back recently on his early work, Heaney has remarked how 'one part of my temperament took over: the private County Derry childhood part of myself rather than the slightly aggravated young Catholic male part.'[23] These two poems, with their promise that speech is about to be unclamped, suggest the restoration of the part that had gone underground while he laboured under the influence of Ted Hughes.

If Heaney had begun to recognize the troubling ideological implications of his early work, his friendship with Seamus Deane may have been a factor. The two had been fellow pupils at St Columb's College, Derry, an exclusively Catholic boarding school whose scholarship boys in the 1950s also included the radical Eamonn McCann. Deane had a strong interest in politics as well as literature, and was particularly scathing about poets who went in for 'Irishry' and 'Oirishness'. In his essay 'Irish Poetry and Irish Nationalism', for instance, he argues that 'a reputation for linguistic extravagance is dangerous, especially when given to small nations by a bigger one which dominates them. By means of it, Celts can stay quaint and stay put'.[24] In the changed political climate of Northern Ireland in the late 1960s, when the Catholics, no longer willing to 'stay put', were campaigning for their civil rights, considerations such as these began to seem pertinent: poetry was no longer, as it must have appeared in the more tranquil 1950s and early 1960s, a special preserve. On 5 October 1968, in Derry, civil rights marchers campaigning for 'One Man One Vote' clashed with the Royal Ulster Constabulary, and the subsequent riots were widely seen on British television. This was not, as it turned out, the spirit of '1968' and world revolution, but rather the beginning of the present wave of Northern Irish Troubles and of violence which by the end of 1969 had led to the mobilizing of the B-Specials, the calling in of British troops, the formation of the Provisional wing of the IRA, and rioting in Belfast so intense that nearly 2000 families fled their homes.

Heaney's attitudes to these events are not widely known, and it is generally assumed that he preferred to 'stay out of politics'. But he had, in fact, been a determined campaigner for civil rights, taking part in marches and being moved by the Derry clashes to write, on 24 October 1968: 'Two years ago, in an article on Belfast, I tried to present both sides as more or less blameworthy. But it seems now that the Catholic minority in Northern Ireland at large, if it is to retain any self-respect, will have to risk the charge of wrecking the new moderation and seek justice more vociferously.'[25] The Derry clashes also moved Heaney to write a polemical ballad, which seems to have circulated as samizdat. The poem is a harsh, ironic piece purporting to come from the Loyalist side but calculated to stir Catholic solidarity:

Come all ye Ulster loyalists and in full chorus join,
Think on the deeds of Craig's Dragoons who strike below
    the groin,
And drink a toast to the truncheon and the armoured
    water-hose
That mowed a swathe through Civil Rights and spat on
    Papish clothes. . . .

O William Craig, you are our love, our lily and our sash,
You have the boys who fear no noise, who'll batter and
    who'll bash.
They'll cordon and they'll baton charge, they'll silence pro-
    test tunes,
They are the hounds of Ulster, boys, sweet William Craig's
    Dragoons.[26]

Heaney did not publish or put his name to this poem: he had no desire to become known as a propagandist. But the events of 1968–9 did exhilarate him – 'There was an energy and excitement and righteousness in the air at that time, by people like myself who hadn't always been political'[27] – and changed his notion of what his poetry should be doing: 'From that moment the problems of poetry moved from being simply a matter of achieving the satisfactory verbal icon to being a search for images and symbols adequate to our predicament' (*P*, p. 56).

If *Wintering Out* (1972) bears the first real fruits of that search, this is not to imply the two earlier books had been entirely lacking in political awareness. 'At a Potato Digging' and 'For the Commander of the Eliza' had referred back to the Great Famine of 1845; 'Requiem for the Croppies' was about the rebellion of 1798; 'Docker' had warned, about sectarian violence, 'Oh yes, that kind of thing could start again'. Nor would it be true to say that the poems of *Wintering Out* are explicitly 'about' what Heaney lived through in Belfast in the late 1960s: only 'A Northern Hoard', with its references to 'gunshot, siren and clucking gas', is a poem of historical witness, and then only shadowily (it works through dream and nightmare). What *Wintering Out* does is to explore the deeper structures of present hostilities, the way in which the divisions of the Protestant and Catholic communities are embedded in language and topography. Lovingly dwelling on place, name and place-name, he continues to draw from a rich store of personal memory, but also opens up much wider perspectives of history.

Heaney does not leave the territory of his childhood, then, but returns to it with new eyes and ears. Naming the places of his youth – Anahorish, Moyola, Toome, Broagh, Derrygarve, and so on – allows him, as before, to recall a world of lushness and delight: 'the windy boortrees / and rhubarb-blades' (*WO*, p. 27), 'the shiny grass / and darkened cobbles / in the bed of the lane' (*WO*, p. 16). But it is also an enunciation of divided cultural experience. Mossbawn, the Heaney family's farm in Derry until they moved when he was fourteen, interests him here not because of its idyllic 'sunlit yard' (the image occurs in both *Death of a Naturalist* and his later volume *North*) but because of its hybrid name – 'moss' being a Norse or Viking word used by the Irish to mean 'bog', 'bawn' being an English or Scottish word for 'fort' – and because of its location: lying

39

between Toome Bridge and Castledawson, it suggests to Heaney 'a symbolic placing for a Northern Catholic, to be in-between the marks of nationalist local sentiment on the one hand, and the marks of colonial and British presence on the other'.[28] Pronunciation of local names and words is a key to caste: *fodder* – 'Or, as we said, / *fother*' (*WO*, p. 13); *Broagh* – with 'that last / *gh* the strangers found / difficult to manage' (*WO*, p. 27); *the wool trade* – 'the phrase / Rambled warm as a fleece / Out of his hoard' (*WO*, p. 37). After the tight gag of the earlier books comes a proliferation of direct speech and of images of the tongue – 'the civil tongues', 'that tongue of chosen people', 'the gallery of the tongue', 'river tongues', 'the swinging tongue of his body'. And, as the poet strains to catch the intonations of speech, there is a new emphasis on the ear: 'I lie with my ear / in this loop of silence' (*WO*, p. 22); 'I cock my ear / at an absence' (*WO*, p. 24). Formerly wary of sound, he becomes what he calls a 'lobe and larynx / of the mossy places' (*WO*, p. 28), listening to and trying for himself the accents of the tribe.

Heaney's interest in dialect and pronunciation had begun much earlier when, as a student at Queen's University, he attended the English-language lectures of John Braidwood and G. B. Adams. These two were later the driving forces behind a book called *Ulster Dialects: An Introductory Symposium* (1964), which considered such matters as the relationship between Ulster dialect and Elizabethan English ('some cherished archaisms / are correct Shakespearean', as Heaney himself put it in *Wintering Out* (p. 31)). This book may well have influenced Heaney, for it used technical terms like *spirant*, *plosive* and *fricative* which he incorporated into his work, and it concerned itself with what one contributor calls 'a dialect boundary in the English of Ireland [referring] back to an ancient political (and racial) division'.[29] In its meticulous examination of the relationship between language and land, *Ulster Dialects* encouraged Heaney to become a 'fieldworker' in the archives of grammar and pronunciation.

Place-names, as the most obvious example of land-language, have a special fascination for Heaney. Anahorish, Antrim, Aran, Ardboe Point, Ballymurphy, Ballyshannon, Beldberg, Belmullet, Boyne, Brandon, Brandywell, Broagh, Carrickfergus, Castledawson, Cavehill, Church Island, Coleraine, Derrygarve, Devenish, Donegal, Drogheda, Dunseverick, Fews Forest, Glanmore, Gweebarra, Horse Island, Kildare, Lough Beg, Lough Neagh, Malin, Mayo, Moher, Moyola, Newtownhamilton, Newry, Portstewart, Slane, Smerwick, Strangford, Tory, Upperlands, Ventry, Vinegar Hill, Westport, Wicklow: an astonishing number of place-names are dotted about his work and make a good, large-scale map of Ireland a useful thing to have to hand when reading him. In its preoccupation with place-names, his poetry might be thought to belong to the tradition of *dinnseanches*, Celtic poems and tales which, as Heaney says, 'relate the original meanings of place-names and constitute a form of mythological etymology' (*P*, p. 131). But Heaney's is more a political etymology, its accents those of sectarianism. From its burrowing in place-names and in the ancient 'word hoard' it uncovers a history of linguistic and territorial dispossession. The hard, masculine, consonantal language of England has invaded and displaced the soft, fluid, feminine language of the Gaelic vowel:

> Our guttural muse
> was bulled long ago
> by the alliterative tradition,
> her uvula grows
>
> vestigial, forgotten
> like the coccyx
> or a Brigid's Cross
> yellowing in some outhouse . . . (*WO*, p. 31)

Heaney's tone here is elegiac, seemingly resigned to English sovereignty; elsewhere it is actively placatory, as in 'The Other Side', where he patiently gropes to understand the language and customs of his Protestant neighbour. But one poem, 'A

41

New Song', toys subversively with the possibility of some kind of repossession. Hearing the place-name 'Derrygarve', the poet is transported back to his colourful Arcadian childhood: 'A kingfisher's blue bolt at dusk / And stepping stones like black molars / Sunk in the ford'. The tone is again nostalgic: the name Derrygarve seems 'a lost potent musk', 'Vanished music, twilit water, / A smooth libation of the past', soothing but remote. In the last two stanzas, however, the tone changes abruptly as the poet envisages a retrieval and advance:

> But now our river tongues must rise
> From licking deep in native haunts
> To flood, with vowelling embrace,
> Demesnes staked out in consonants.
>
> And Castledawson we'll enlist
> And Upperlands, each planted bawn –
> Like bleaching-greens resumed by grass –
> A vocable, as rath and bullaun. (*WO*, p. 33)

Heaney here addresses the territorial imperative. But the ambiguity in that word 'must' – does it mean 'ought to' or 'will inevitably'? – makes it difficult to decide whether the poem is an urgent call to action or a dispassionate prophecy. A period of insularity (of 'licking deep in native haunts') is declared over: Gaelic vowels will be united with English consonants to form 'vocables'; the bawns, demesnes and bleaching-greens of the Protestant planters will be 'resumed' by Northern Catholics. But Heaney is hazy about how such a realignment is to be carried out: the word 'embrace', with its associations of harmony and lovemaking, implies that it may be done peacefully; the verbs 'flood' and 'enlist', on the other hand, suggest a more forceful and even violent kind of takeover; and the word 'resumed' (given over to? shared with? repossessed by?) is suitably noncommittal. It is a difficult poem, but its difficulties arise, more than anything, from Heaney's uncertainty about where he stands. Choosing to face important cultural questions head-on, he then finds himself wanting to sidestep them.

His better place-name poems work more obliquely and intuitively, without that sense of strain. There is 'Toome', for example, a short enough poem to quote in full:

> My mouth holds round
> the soft blastings,
> *Toome, Toome,*
> as under the dislodged
>
> slab of the tongue
> I push into a souterrain
> prospecting what new
> in a hundred centuries'
>
> loam, flints, musket-balls,
> fragmented ware,
> torcs and fish-bones
> till I am sleeved in
>
> alluvial mud that shelves
> suddenly under
> bogwater and tributaries,
> and elvers tail my hair. (*WO*, p. 26)

There could hardly be a more graphic illustration of the part that 'saying aloud' has come to play in Heaney's poetry. To pronounce the word 'Toome', as one can verify by doing it oneself, it is necessary to move the lips forward and to lift the tongue. Heaney imagines this as a process whereby the potentially blocking 'slab' of the tongue is dislodged, enabling the poet to burrow down beyond fluency and the politer conventions of speech to what he calls elsewhere his 'guttural muse'. This action of digging or 'prospecting' (the 'soft blastings' of pronunciation are like explosions which open up a valuable mine) reveals the buried matter of history – 'loam, flints, musket-balls / fragmented ware, / torcs and fish-bones'. Other Heaney poems have similar lists of archaeological finds – 'flint and iron, / Cast-offs, scraps, nail, canine' (*WO*, p. 44); 'antler combs, bone pins, / coins, weights, scale-pans' (*N*, p. 22). The significance of the finds in this poem is that, first, they are turned up in a souterrain (not just a synonym for 'subterranean' but a word referring specifically to the underground chambers scattered in their thousands about Ireland, often associated with ancient burial mounds and occasionally used to store away smuggled goods and arms) and that, second, they recede and descend through time – from the 'loam' of the recent past, through the 'musket-balls' used by the British military during late eighteenth-century skirmishes (Toome Bridge was the scene of one such skirmish, the place where the Irish nationalist Rody McCorley was hanged in 1798), to the 'torcs' (neckwear) of the ancient Irish. The 'alluvial mud' and 'bog-water' in the last stanza indicate that the poet, having tunnelled back and down through a 'hundred centuries', has reached the primeval source of his selfhood and race. The final Medusa-like image has echoes of evolution theory (man and mammals having been preceded by fish and reptiles) or may be intended to suggest that the poet has restored contact with what he has described as the valuable 'life-forces' that prevailed in Ireland before Saint Patrick banished the snakes.[30] It certainly owes something to Celtic myth: Anne Ross's *Pagan Celtic Britain* (1967), a book Heaney has admitted to being familiar with (*P*, p. 59), has excellent illustrations of the Gorgon or Medusa heads popular in Celtic Britain and Ireland, one of which indeed looks 'elvered'.[31] The image, at any rate, declares that the poet has located his primeval, preliterate self and 'guttural muse' (the poem of this title in *Field Work* is similarly preoccupied with fishes and mud). He has done so not by leaving his native ground but by looking into it more deeply; he chooses excavation rather than exile.

The notion of excavation had, of course, been present in Heaney's work from the very first, with 'Digging'. But there were at this stage two important developments of the idea. One came about through his experiment with a poetic form he thought more suited to this kind of archaeology: compressed, mostly two-stress lines, unrhymed, arranged in slender quatrains, and having an extremely narrow appearance on the page. Some of William Carlos Williams's and Robert Creeley's poetry looks rather like this, and Heaney had read their work while in California in 1969–70. He thought of the form, which dominates *Wintering Out* and *North*, as nurturing his 'arterial' imagination: the poems are to be seen as drills, wells, augers, capillaries, mine-shafts, bore-holes, plumb-lines. These analogies might appear rather fanciful; and there is no self-evident reason why the form in itself should enable a poet to go 'more deeply' into his subject. But it does seem to have served this purpose for Heaney. The rhyming quatrains and pentameters of his early work had forced him into a superficial rationalist mode: the wide lines and blockish stanzas lie like planks boarding up the well of his imagination. Now, as the downward movement of 'Toome' demonstrates, he began to draw on previously repressed psychic and mythic material. There are still in *Wintering Out* some uncertainties about handling the form (can the line 'your trail. Your trail' from 'Servant Boy' really be considered a line?), but by the time of *North* most of these have disappeared.

Another important dimension was added by Heaney's growing fascination with the peat-bog. Peat has unique preservative properties which make the bog a kind of 'memory bank' retaining the evidence of past cultures and civilizations. Heaney's new verse-form imitates the bog, its lines like layers of history, its structure an attempt to keep the past alive. Here again, E. Estyn Evans may have been an influence on Heaney's development: his *Irish Folk Ways* pays attention to the bog, speaking of it as 'an approximate chronological sequence of landscapes and human culture going back several thousand years' and recounting the recovery from Irish bogs of perfectly preserved butter.[32] The fine poem 'Bogland', which concludes *Door into the Dark* and points forward to *Wintering Out*, enlarges on the bog butter recoveries:

Butter sunk under
More than a hundred years
Was recovered salty and white.
The ground itself is kind, black butter

Melting and opening underfoot,
Missing its last definition
By millions of years. (*DD*, p. 55)

But in 1969 a book appeared with more spectacular evidence of peat preservation. P. V. Glob's *The Bog People* tells of the discovery in Danish bogs of a number of remarkably intact human bodies dating back to the Iron Age and evidently the sacrificial victims of an ancient northern religion. Glob's account, though diligently scientific (full of carbon dating, radiographs, and analysis of stomach contents), is vivid and powerful, and Heaney admired its 'piety towards objects': 'When I read [Glob] . . . I experience feelings normally evinced by the charms of poetry itself.'[33] Heaney has said that it was the photographs in Glob's book, rather than the prose, which made the greatest impact on him, but seven of the eight bog poems he wrote are closely related to passages from *The Bog People*: 'The Tollund Man' (pp. 21–32), 'Nerthus' (p. 26), 'The Grauballe Man' (pp. 33–48), 'Come to the Bower' (pp. 58–63), 'Bog Queen' (pp. 77–8), 'Punishment' and 'Strange Fruit' (pp. 83–4 and 114).[34] Of the Tollund Man Heaney writes, 'Some day I will go to Aarhus / To see his peat-brown head' (*WO*, p. 47): interestingly, it was not until 1973 that he made this journey, by which time his bog poems were written. It was the skilful narrative and excellent photographs in Glob's book, rather than the Danish museum exhibits, which fired his imagination.

The bog poems loom less largely in *Wintering Out* than in *North*, where there are more of them (six rather than two) and where they are assumed within the framework of a comprehensive historical myth. But 'The Tollund Man' shows that Heaney believed from the beginning that some kind of connection exists between Iron Age sacrifices to the Mother Goddess of Earth and the violent history of Northern Ireland. Description of the corpse in Part I of this poem is followed by a reference in Part II to an outrage apparently committed by B-Specials in the 1920s ('four young brothers, trailed / For miles along the lines'; *WO*, p. 48) and by a hint in Part III as to the troubling familiarity of ancient sacrificial practices:

> Out there in Jutland
> In the old man-killing parishes
> I will feel lost,
> Unhappy and at home. (*WO*, p. 48)

This crossing of the 'man-killing parishes' of the distant past with those of the neighbourly present anticipates the methods of *North*.

Heaney's new-found ability to allow historical, political, linguistic and mythological material to overlap and interpenetrate makes the first half of *Wintering Out* one of the high points of his career: 'Bog Oak', 'Anahorish', 'Toome', 'Broagh', 'Gifts of Rain', 'The Backward Look', 'Traditions', 'The Tollund Man' – these are among the finest examples of his work. The place-name poems, in particular, helped resolve the divided loyalties of his early work, as he has himself explained:

> I had a great sense of release as they were being written, a joy and devil-may-careness, and that convinced me that one could be faithful to the nature of the English language – for in some senses these poems are erotic mouth-music by and out of the anglo-saxon tongue – and, at the same time, be faithful to one's own non-English origin, for me that is County Derry.[35]

As Heaney goes on to say, the difficulty is in repeating such liberating experience, and it must be said that after these poems Part Two of *Wintering Out* comes as disappointment. It consists chiefly of poems either about marriage, memorable only for the occasional image ('Our love calls tiny as a tuning fork' (*WO*, p. 61); 'as you bend in the shower / water lives down the tilting stoups of your breasts' (*WO*, p. 60)), or about real or mythical women associated with sea and with the night; and it concludes with the vaguely portentous 'Westering', an unholy mix of Easter symbolism, moon imagery and the poet's departure from Ireland to California. The falling off in quality reminds us that, whatever the strength of the individual poems in *Wintering Out*, Heaney was still some way short of compiling a unified book that could sustain its interest right to the end: only with *North* and *Field Work* was he able to do that.

*

In the meantime, however, he was at work on another enterprise. In 1970–1, while in California, he made a start on the poems that were to form the little-known *Stations*. This collection of twenty-one short pieces returned once again to experiences from the poet's childhood, but in a new form (short prose-paragraphs) and with what the Preface describes as 'the excitement of coming for the first time to a place I had always known completely' (*S*, p. 3). Heaney's return to a troubled Belfast prevented him from finishing these poems until the summer of 1974. They were finally published by Frank Ormsby the following year.

The collection is at once more oblique and more direct than anything Heaney had so far written. Some of the obscurities come from the very local nature of the material: 'The stations of the west' cannot be understood without knowing that Northern Irish Catholic teenagers are often sent to Donegal during the summer vacation in order to learn Gaelic; 'Ballad' is based on a ballad about a 1950s political killing. Other pieces are so abstruse that they need corresponding pieces or reworkings to explain them. The 'helmeted pump' in 'Sinking the shaft' turns up again in the first poem of *North*; the phrases 'exhaustion . . . nominated peace' and 'I crept before I walked' are re-employed to better effect in *North* and *Field Work*;

'Cauled', about the experience of being lost as a child, is elucidated by a similar passage in *Preoccupations*:

> They thought he was lost. For years they talked about it until he found himself at the root of their kindly tongues, sitting like a big fieldmouse in the middle of the rig. Their voices were far-off now, searching something.
>
> Green air trawled over his arms and legs, the pods and stalks wore a fuzz of light. He caught a rod in each hand and jerked the whole tangle into life. Little tendrils unsprung, new veins lit in the shifting leaves, a caul of shadows stretched and netted round his head again. He sat listening, grateful as the calls encroached.
>
> They had found him at first onset of sobbing. (*S*, p. 4)

> I do not know what age I was when I got lost in the pea-drills in a field behind the house, but it is a half-dream to me, and I've heard about it so often that I may even be imagining it. Yet, by now, I have imagined it so long and so often that I know what it was like: a green web, a caul of veined light, a tangle of rods and pods, stalks and tendrils, full of assuaging earth and leaf smell, a sunlit lair. I'm sitting as if just wakened from a winter sleep and gradually become aware of voices, coming closer, calling my name, and for no reason at all I have begun to weep. (*P*, p. 17)

Heaney, we can see, has a clear sense of the difference between prose and prose-poetry. There are common images here – pods, stalks, tendrils, leaves, light – but the first passage is altogether more mysterious. It withholds circumstantial information about 'where' and 'when'; its metaphors ('he found himself at the root of their kindly tongues', 'green air trawled over his arms and legs') are more ambitious; and it evokes with greater resonance a kind of womb-like, pantheistic intimacy between the boy and his green surroundings. The poem is the first one in *Stations*, and the image of the caul (a part of the placenta that sometimes envelops children's heads at birth) and

49

'the first onset of sobbing' suggest that it is intended to record a kind of birth. It is powerful but almost too obscure; one is grateful that a prose translation exists.

Heaney himself has acknowledged the justice of the criticism that these poems 'aren't realized or thrown free, that they are like private family memories, pious.'[36] But some of the images of schooldays are accessible enough (chalk, milk-bottle tops, a bean in a jamjar that has 'split its sides' – the atmosphere is like that of Joyce's Clongowes), and there is a very striking use of period detail to suggest Ireland during the Second World War: bombers flying overhead, Haw-Haw broadcasts being enthusiastically received in Catholic homes, a German POW walking up the fields, Heaney's father nervously exchanging jokes with a demobbed Protestant neighbour who has brought him back some rosary beads ('I stole them for you, Paddy, off the pope's dresser when his back was turned'). The solid historical element in *Stations* not only restrains the more dangerously recondite and indulgent elements in the poet's self-mythologizing but shows his childhood territory to be intensely politicized, as it was not in *Death of a Naturalist* and *Door into the Dark* but had begun to be in *Wintering Out*. There are poems referring to Orange drummers, to the sabotage by Protestants of a Gaelic football game, and to the unpleasant (for Heaney) English royalist associations of the name of the flower 'Sweet William'. At times, as in 'Kernes', the childhood sectarianism looks a little contrived:

> Candystriped red, white and blue, ringed with influence like a fairy thorn, the newly painted flagpole cut the wind. With his hand to its true wood, Dixon balanced upright on the bicycle, a saddled declamatory king of the castle.
>
> 'I could beat every fucking papish in the school!'
>
> We piled our schoolbags at a distance, defied from sanctuary, and began to tear a small arsenal of sods from the green verge. The bicycle, with its crome insignia and rivetted breastplate of Sir Walter Raleigh in his inflated knickers, motioned.

'No surrender! Up King Billy every time!'

He came through us with his head sunk and the pedals flying and further down the road was standing to on the first bar of their yard gate, singing 'God Save the King'.

One by one we melted down lanes and over pads, behind a glib he hadn't even ruffled. (*S*, p. 14)

The problem is not that the incident rings untrue (Heaney speaks of it again in an interview)[37] but that the children are too calculatingly employed to act out larger adult themes. The poem has the air of being deliberately thought out – its symbolism (the 'breastplate of Sir Walter Raleigh' on the bicycle, for example) over-explicit, its revival of the ancient Irish word 'glib' (meaning thick, matted hair) conspicuous, the narrative generally dominated by a prearranged scheme. Another way of putting this would be to say that the poem is *faux-naïf*, its authorial consciousness too far in advance of the narrative voice.

An awareness of such limitations may be one of the reasons why Heaney chose to publish *Stations* in modest pamphlet form and to include nothing from it when assembling his *Selected Poems*. There was also the consideration that some of his narrator's quasi-chivalric boastings ('I was champion of the examination halls, scalding with lust inside my daunting visor', 'I have wandered far from that ring-giver and would not renegue on this migrant solitude') sounded uncannily like those of Offa in Geoffrey Hill's *Mercian Hymns*, a prose-poem collection which appeared in 1973; after the advances of *Wintering Out*, it would have set Heaney back to be accused once again of imitating his English contemporaries. He knew, besides, that in the poems he'd written between about 1971 and 1974 he had the basis of a strong and distinctive book. These poems were collected under the title *North* and published in June 1975.

4

THE GROUND POSSESSED: 'NORTH'

The propagandist, whether moral or political, complains that the writer should use his power over words to persuade people to a particular course of action, instead of fiddling while Rome burns. But Poetry is not concerned with telling people what to do, but with extending our knowledge of good and evil, perhaps making the necessity for action more urgent and its nature more clear, but only leading us to the point where it is possible for us to make a rational and moral choice. (W. H. Auden, *The Poet's Tongue*)

Up until *North* (1975) Seamus Heaney had been content to publish books that were little more than a string of individual lyrics, collections that had 'meanings' but no overall 'meaning'. His interest in the structure of his collections had been at best perfunctory: aside from dividing *Wintering Out* into two parts, and from allowing the last poems of one book to point forward to the concerns of the next, he had not exploited the possibilities of strategic arrangement. By the mid-1970s, however, Heaney had begun to look towards the more ambitious design and larger sweep of epic poetry, and in particular to long Irish poems which addressed themselves to nothing less than the history of the nation. Two recent publications encouraged him in this: Thomas Kinsella's translation of the eighth-century Ulster epic *The Tain*, in 1970,[38] and John Montague's ambitious 'image of Ireland' *The Rough Field*, in 1973,[39] a sequence subtitled 'Ulster 1961–1971' but drawing on sources going back to the sixteenth century. Moreover, Heaney himself had been translating *Buile Shuibhne*, a Middle Irish romance about the northern king, Sweeney, which also confronted the matter of nationhood. The influence of these long poems is certainly discernible in *North*. Though still using lyric forms and anxious not to let 'the mythic scheme dominate the private felicities and discoveries of the everyday occasional things',[40] he took great pains over the book's arrangement, revising a number of pieces after their original magazine publication and treating the poems less as independent wholes than as contributions to an unfolding argument. In *North*, it is scarcely an exaggeration to say, the structure of the book is its meaning: the placing and interlocking of the poems amount to the creation of a historical myth.

Heaney's new attention to structure, which was certainly nurtured by his becoming a full-time writer in 1972, is most obviously discernible in his division of *North* into two distinct but complementary parts. In Part I the 'North' explored is northern Europe over the last 2000 years; the dominant verse-form is the compressed, 'artesian' quatrain already employed in *Wintering Out*; the tone is reverential, formal, serious; and the language is deeply rooted in the past, to the extent of reviving defunct and archaic words. In Part II 'North' means contemporary Northern Ireland; the dominant verse-form is the rhyming quatrain in iambic pentameters; the tone is conversational, irreverent, humorous; and the language is contemporary and at times journalistic. Concerning itself with a divided culture, *North* is at odds with itself – but fruitfully so.

The binary structure of *North* is more, however, than an example of 'form' reflecting 'content': it satisfies a temperamental need in Heaney. His essays, reviews and interviews repeatedly advance the idea that there are two kinds of poetry and two kinds of poet: *les vers donnés* as against *les vers calculés*; the poetry of chance and trance as against the poetry of resistance and perseverance; the poetry of 'sinking in' or the poetry of 'coming up against'; the instinctual or the rational; the feminine or the masculine; the 'artesian' or the 'architec-

tonic'; the epiphanic or the crafted; the 'ooze' of poetry or its
'spur of flame'; the 'lived, illiterate and unconscious' or the
'learned, literate and conscious'; the takers (Wordsworth,
D. H. Lawrence, Keats, Patrick Kavanagh) and the makers
(Yeats, Hopkins, Jonson, Lowell, John Montague, John
Hewitt); poets who sense, surrender, dive, divine, receive and
coax, or poets who command, plot, assert, strike, labour and
force. These polarities crop up in nearly all the essays in
Heaney's critical book *Preoccupations* and bear some resembl-
ance to Roland Barthes's distinction between *l'écrivain* and
l'écrivant. They are most extensively discussed in 'The Makings of a Music' (on Wordsworth and Yeats) and 'The Fire i' the
Flint' (on Hopkins). At one point Heaney reconciles the two
opposing spirits of poetry – Yeats is said to prove that 'deli-
beration can be so intensified that it becomes synonymous with
inspiration' (*P*, p. 110) – but elsewhere hostilities continue
unabated. What they suggest is that Heaney sees his career as
having fluctuated between two different types of poetic composition, *Death of a Naturalist*, for example, having been
laboured over and 'made', the place-name poems of *Wintering
Out* having been 'given'. The distinction of *North* lies in its
self-conscious incorporation of both kinds of poem, the instinctual mode making up Part I, the rational Part II. As Heaney
himself has said: 'The two halves of the book constitute two
different types of utterance, each of which arose out of a
necessity to shape and give palpable linguistic form to two
kinds of urgency – one symbolic, one explicit.'[41]

If the 'symbolic' mode was a continuation of the work begun
in *Wintering Out*, the 'explicit' was a deliberate response to
historical circumstance. When Heaney returned to Belfast in
the summer of 1971, after a year away in Berkeley, California,
he found that the 'situation' in the North had taken a sharp
turn for the worse. Relations between the Catholic community
and the British soldiers drafted in in 1969 had seriously
deteriorated; the Provisional IRA bombing campaign had been
stepped up; and in August 1971 internment was reintroduced,

leading to the arrest of hundreds of Catholics in a series of dawn raids on Republican homes. 'It hasn't been named martial law but that's what it feels like,' Heaney wrote at Christmas 1971:

Everywhere soldiers with cocked guns are watching you – that's what they're here for – on the streets, at the corners of streets, from doorways, over the puddles on demolished sites. At night jeeps and armoured cars groan past without lights; or road-blocks are thrown up, and once again it's delays measured in hours, searches and signings among the guns and torches. . . . Fear has begun to tingle through the place. Who's to know the next target on the Provisional list? Who's to know the reprisals won't strike where you are? (P, pp. 30–1)

Heaney's prose from this period bears signs of the pressure he was living under: he describes a terrifying dream he had, 'a wounded man falling towards me with his bloodied hands lifted to tear at me or to implore' (P, p. 33). The decent, ameliorist, civil rights mood that had lain behind *Wintering Out* seemed to belong to an earlier period. He felt the need to write poetry that would be not necessarily propagandist but certainly urgent in tone, and 'to take the English lyric and make it eat stuff that it has never eaten before . . . like all the messy, and it would seem incomprehensible obsessions in the North.'[42] His first and principal effort in this vein came in October 1971, when *The Listener* published his documentary sequence about the Troubles, 'Whatever You Say, Say Nothing', in an issue that also included media investigations of 'the Irish thing'. Some of Heaney's lines – 'Men die at hand. In blasted street and home / The gelignite's a common sound effect' – might almost have been taken from the journalistic prose alongside.

The pressure on Heaney came from without, of course, as well as from within. In the early 1970s, in a new version of the old cry 'Where are the war poets?', critics and journalists had begun to call for a poetry that would 'deal with' the Troubles;

and Heaney, as the best-known of the Belfast 'Group', and by now something of a public figure, was particularly subject to such exhortations. Thus when *North* finally appeared in 1975, containing some poems quite explicitly about the Troubles, there was an almost audible sigh of relief. Reviewers spoke of its recognition of 'tragedy and violence'[43] and of its 'testimony to the patience, persistence and power of the imagination under duress'.[44] The book was widely received as Heaney's 'arrival' as an important poet, winning several prizes and selling 6000 copies in its first month. At the same time it was noticeable that, with the exception of Conor Cruise O'Brien in *The Listener*, none of the London reviewers seemed at all clear about what view of the Troubles the volume took or what loyalties it betrayed; it was enough, apparently, that it should be 'involved'. In Belfast, where there was no such doubt about what was being said, the reception of the book was markedly less enthusiastic. In *The Honest Ulsterman* Edna Longley spoke of its 'stylistic inflation' and Ciaran Carson of its 'wrong notions of history'. Carson concluded: 'Everyone was anxious that *North* should be a great book; when it turned out it wasn't, it was treated as one anyway, and made into an Ulster '75 Exhibition of the Good that can come out of Troubled Times.'[45]

Heaney's niggardly representation of *North* in his 1980 *Selected Poems* — only about half the poems are included — suggests that he now inclines more to the Belfast consensus than the London one. Honest doubt about the achievement of the book may be the reason, but it is noticeable that some of the more 'explicit' poems — 'Ocean's Love to Ireland', 'Freedman', 'The Betrothal of Cavehill' and 'Orange Drums, Tyrone, 1966' — are the ones to have been dropped. What this suggests is that Heaney has lost faith in the binary structure originally intended for *North* and has begun to play down its more 'conscious' side. Indeed, even at the time of publication, in a note accompanying the book, he remarked: 'During the last few years there has been considerable expectation that poets from

Northern Ireland should "say" something about "the situation", but in the end they will only be worth listening to if they are saying something about and to themselves.'[46] As a response to journalists determined to treat Ulster poets as mere spokesmen, this is fair and necessary comment. But it does have the effect of throwing weight behind one half of the book, the 'intuitive' Part I; and it is also in danger of being taken as saying that poetry is necessarily the poorer once it begins to sound an explicitly political note. Recent critics have followed Heaney's lead in this: instead of a creative interplay between opposed but complementary modes of utterance, we are encouraged to see *North* as being fatally divided between the 'true' (private, instinctual, historical) poems of Part I and the 'false' (public, willed, contemporary) poems of Part II. We are also encouraged to see Heaney's brief venture into politics as being a mistake: it is no coincidence that the most widely quoted lines from *North* are those where Heaney describes himself as 'neither internee nor informer' but 'a wood-kerne / Escaped from the massacre' (*N*, p. 73); for wrenched from context these lines suggest that Heaney is really a private, neutral and apolitical writer.

But just as the word 'wood-kerne' has quite definite political overtones (wood-kernes were the shadowy Gaelic outlaws who put up resistance to the Protestant colonization of Ireland, and of whom later Republican gangs of 'boys' are the natural successors), so *North* as originally conceived by Heaney was an ambitious historical myth with a quite definite political mission – 'the book all books were leading to', as he once described it.[47] I want here to restore that sense of its importance, and to explain the image of Ireland that it creates. I want, too, to pay attention to the book's structure, which is altogether more complex, and altogether less rigid, than has been supposed: the division between the private and the public, the instinctual and the willed, and so on, is not at all as stable as it might appear.

*

57

The two opening dedicatory 'Mossbawn' pieces illustrate this complexity. Placed outside the main bipartite structure as pieces charming in themselves, they nevertheless introduce the collection's main theme (ancestry, continuity, 'calendar customs'), offering affirmations to be balanced against the bleakness of what follows. 'Sunlight', which describes Heaney's aunt at work, baking, in the kitchen, is on the face of it no more than a memory of and memorial to family and home. But the 'tick of two clocks' is to be heard in it: the timeless final image – 'here is love / like a tinsmith's scoop / sunk past its gleam / in the meal-bin' (*N*, p. 9) – opens the poem out beyond its own ground, discovering beneath the transient gleam of sunlit surfaces the deep common substance of love. In its transcendence of a time-bound domain, 'Sunlight' prepares for the 'anonymities' of its companion piece, 'The Seed Cutters'. These labourers in the fields have 'time to kill' and are 'taking their time', but time does not kill or take them. The persistence of their centuries-old field work gives solace to Heaney in his time much as the 'man harrowing clods' gave solace to Hardy in his ('this will go onward the same / Though dynasties pass'). Like Hardy, Heaney discovers a world beyond war's annals; unlike him, he taxes himself with the issue of artistic composition – there is the problem of how to 'get them true' and how to 'compose the frieze / With all of us there' (*N*, p. 10). In this self-consciousness about the poet's relationship to his people and to his time, Heaney again prepares the ground for the main body of his book.

Part I of *North* begins and ends with poems based on the Antaeus myth. Containing the other poems like book-ends, these two pieces can be read as both artistic and political allegories. As the former they express the quarrel in Heaney between the instinctual (Antaeus) and the rational (Hercules): Antaeus prevails in Part I of *North*, so that Hercules' victory over him is a necessary prelude to the 'declarative' mode of Part II.[48] Politically, these are poems about colonization, suggesting that dispossession is the inevitable lot of small, backward nations. In the first poem ('Antaeus') the dark, native Antaeus, whose survival depends on staying close to the soil, maintains his position of strength and independence, convinced that he 'cannot be weaned / Off the earth's long contour' (N, p. 12). In the second poem ('Hercules and Antaeus') Hercules, 'royal' invader, hero of light and technology, 'his mind big with golden apples, / his future hung with trophies', defeats Antaeus by lifting him into the air and thereby banishing him to 'a dream of loss / and origins' (N, p. 52): Antaeus' elevation is his fall. One could read this as an allegory of the Protestant settlement of Ireland. But it is more a parable of imperialism generally, referring to defeated Anglo-Saxon and Red Indian heroes as well as to an ancient Irish one – 'Balor will die / and Byrthnoth and Sitting Bull' (N, p. 53).

The imagery in the second of these two poems – a 'spur of light' defeating the 'black powers' of earth, the 'sky-born' dispossessing the 'mould-hugger', Ariel ousting Caliban – suggests the influence of writers like Pablo Neruda and Edward Brathwaite, whose poems about colonization draw on a similar dialectic of darkness and light. More broadly, the poem owes something to Heaney's year in Berkeley, where, as he recalls, political solidarity with Antaeus was strong:

The whole atmosphere in Berkeley was politicized and minorities like the Chicanos and Blacks were demanding their say. There was a strong sense of contemporary American poetry in the West with Robert Duncan and Bly and Gary Snyder rejecting the intellectual, ironical, sociological idiom of poetry and going for the mythological. I mean everyone wanted to be a Red Indian, basically. And that meshed with my own concerns for I could see a close connection between the political and cultural assertions being made at the time by the minority in the north of Ireland and the protests and consciousness-raising that were going on in the Bay Area. And the poets were a part of this and also, pre-eminently, part of the protest against the Vietnam war. So that was probably the most important influence I came under in Berkeley, that awareness that poetry was a force, almost a mode of power, certainly a mode of resistance.[49]

Though Heaney did bring to *North* this notion of poetry as a 'mode of resistance', it is noticeable that 'Hercules and Antaeus' itself is far from being a poem of protest. Heaney's sympathies undoubtedly lie with the 'minority' represented by Antaeus, but his sense of history tells him that it must always be defeated: 'Balor will die' – the future tense makes the tone of this poem all the more fatalistic.

Framed as they are by the Antaeus legend, the rest of the poems in Part I of *North* must be read within its narrative of invasion and dispossession. They deal with different periods of Irish and northern European history – Celtic rituals, Viking raids, Danish sacrifices, Elizabethan colonizings, the 'Act of Union' – and move chronologically towards the present day. In the first group of six poems, Heaney is again the archaeologist-cum-etymologist of *Wintering Out*: he delves into 'philology and kennings', excavates 'stone-age fields' and allows the incised lines on Viking trial-pieces to lead his own lines of thought. Instructed to 'Lie down / in the word-hoard', he retrieves an extraordinary number of linguistic finds, many of them of Gaelic origin: *glib, corbelled, dulse, althing, bleb, hurdle, haggers, gombeen-men, pampooties, slobland, scop, coulter, gorget, pash, midden, felloes, crannog, holm-gang, obols, pash, quern, ban-hus*. And, doubling his efforts in 'the coffered riches of grammar', he comes up with some coinages of his own, noun compounded on noun: *love-den, blood-holt, dream-bower, oak-bone, bone-vault, sun-bank, brain-firkin, moon-drinker, earth-pantry, mushroom-flesh, ringlet-breath*.

Heaney is aware of the charge that there is perhaps something unhealthy about this constant brooding on dead languages and cultures. He answers it through self-caricature, dramatizing himself as the most famous dramatic character of them all:

I am Hamlet the Dane,
skull-handler, parablist,
smeller of rot

in the state, infused
with its poisons,
pinioned by ghosts
and affections,

murders and pieties,
coming to consciousness
by jumping in graves,
dithering, blathering. (*N*, p. 23)

Posturing though he may seem here, Heaney defends his morbid preoccupations as a way of 'coming to consciousness': this isn't death for death's sake but a way of understanding present lives. The Vikings, with their feuds and grudges, their 'hatreds and behindbacks', are far from remote: the poet addresses them as 'old fathers' and they in turn, 'buoyant with hindsight', provide moral and aesthetic guidance – 'Keep your eye clear / as the bleb of the icicle,' they tell him (*N*, p. 20). The theme of all these poems is 'persistence / A congruence of lives': the past is not another country but a neighbouring field.

The best of this group of poems, 'Funeral Rites', is also the one in which the past most explicitly informs the present. The rituals the poet recalls from the funerals of his childhood are Catholic ones (rosary beads, candles, dressed nail-heads) and thus part of the Christian sectarianism which lies behind the violent deaths of the North – 'as news comes in / of each neighbourly murder' (*N*, p. 16). His desire to revive ancient pagan burial rituals, 'the great chambers of Boyne', is an attempt to recover pre-Christian symbols which would be acceptable to both castes: he imagines these funeral ceremonies as something in which everyone might join, 'the cud of memory / allayed for once'. Carefully preparing the way with Nordic imagery ('igloo brows', 'the black glacier / of each funeral'),

Heaney draws on Icelandic sagas to suggest that death in such circumstances might be 'beautiful', as Gunnar's was:

> Men said that he was chanting
> verses about honour
> and that four lights burned
>
> in corners of the chamber:
> which opened then, as he turned
> with a joyful face
> to look at the moon. (*N*, p. 18)

This is not a world in which murder no longer exists – Gunnar lies 'dead by violence / and unavenged' – but where burial ground might at least be common ground, mourning a 'slow triumph' to be shared by all. The poem is assuaging and uplifting without being idealistic about the prospects of peace in life; and it is certainly as 'public' as anything to be found in Part II of *North*.

   In the next group of six poems Heaney returns to the Bog People, and in particular to their women. His pure fascination with them is impure, sexual, necrophiliac. The bog becomes a love-bower, its female corpses 'insatiable' brides who lie in waiting for an awakening kiss. The poet, unable in his previous books to write love poems for the living, is here a princely seducer of the dead, unpinning and unwrapping, foraging for the 'Venus bone', the word 'love' constantly on his lips ('I love this turf-face', 'I love the spring', 'My poor scapegoat / I almost love you'). But the arrangement of the poems emphasizes a gradual mastery of, and even a sense of guilt about, such feelings. The girl in 'Strange Fruit', with her terrible appearance ('broken nose', 'eyeholes blank as pools', 'beheaded'), rebukingly outstares 'What had begun to feel like reverence'; and 'Kinship' moves from the present tense into the past, the switch suggesting that the poet has gradually outgrown his deification of the dead. For his fascination with their terrible beauty has indeed been a kind of sickness or love-sickness, a symptom not of mere respect for the past's example but of a dangerous obsession with its brutal laws. The initial interest in P. V. Glob's book about the Bog People may have been innocent enough, but Heaney knows that behind these poems lies a disquieting analogy, which he has explained as follows:

> You have a society in the Iron Age where there was ritual blood-letting. You have a society where girls' heads were shaved for adultery, you have a religion centring on the territory, on a goddess of the ground and of the land, and associated with sacrifice. Now in many ways the fury of Irish Republicanism is associated with a religion like this, with a female goddess who has appeared in various guises. She appears as Cathleen ni Houlihan in Yeats's plays; she appears as Mother Ireland. I think that the Republican ethos is a feminine religion, in a way. It seems to me that there are satisfactory imaginative parallels between this religion and time and our own time. They are observed with amazement and a kind of civilised tut-tut by Tacitus in the first century AD and by leader-writers in the Daily Telegraph in the 20th century.[50]

This equation of the Iron Age and the IRA is briefly made at the end of 'The Grauballe Man', where the 'hooded victim, / slashed and dumped' (N, p. 36) might belong either to the past or to the present. 'Punishment' explores the analogy more fully, describing a girl who has been hanged, and her body thrown into the bog, as a punishment for committing adultery. The poem again involves an element of courtship: the 'amber beads' of the girl's nipples, 'the frail rigging / of her ribs', and her 'beautiful' features are attractive to the poet. But he is more here than merely an 'artful voyeur'. The girl's 'tar-black' face and 'shaved head' link her in his mind with the 'betraying sisters' of present-day Northern Ireland, Catholic girls who have been shaved, tarred and feathered by the IRA as a punishment for 'informing' or for going out with British soldiers. Heaney's feelings about this are ambivalent: he pities the victims of such brutal treatment, but his pity is offset and finally outweighed by his understanding of the motives for judicial punishment:

> I who have stood dumb
> when your betraying sisters,
> cauled in tar,
> wept by the railings,
>
> who would connive
> in civilized outrage
> yet understand the exact
> and tribal, intimate revenge. (*N*, p. 38)

'At one minute', Heaney wrote from Belfast in 1972, 'you are drawn towards the old vortex of racial and religious instinct, at another time you seek the mean of humane love and reason' (*P*, p. 34). In this poem the word 'connive' decisively tips the balance, suggesting that Heaney's civilized outrage – the kind of response he describes in Part II of *North*: ' "Oh, it's disgraceful, surely, I agree," / "Where's it going to end?" "It's getting worse" ' (*N*, p. 58) – is forced and artificial in comparison with his instinctive understanding of the laws and needs of the tribe. It is a courageous piece of self-analysis, acknowledging what he calls elsewhere 'the persistence of what appear to be anachronistic passions'.[51] It is also very reminiscent of 'The Early Purges' from *Death of a Naturalist*, where pity for drowned victims is similarly overruled by the adult voice of necessity.

The final four poems (before 'Hercules and Antaeus') in Part I of *North* are about Anglo-Irish relations, and they are united by the metaphor of sexual union. Congress is violent in all cases: one a rape, one presided over by a gun ('The Betrothal of Cavehill'), one resulting in an aggressive offspring, and the other ('Aisling') bringing about the man's destruction. The first of these, 'Ocean's Love to Ireland' (the title an echo of Ralegh's poem to Queen Elizabeth, 'The Ocean's Love to Cynthia'), most fully exploits the play on the word 'possession':

Speaking broad Devonshire,
Ralegh has backed the maid to a tree
As Ireland is backed to England

And drives inland
Till all her strands are breathless:
'Sweesir, Swatter! Sweesir, Swatter!' (*N*, p. 46)

Heaney omits this poem from his *Selected Poems*, perhaps on
the grounds that it is too knowingly constructed, especially
when compared to its companion piece set in the same period,
'Bog Oak' from *Wintering Out*. Certainly its compacting of the
historical, geographical, sexual and linguistic is dense and
deliberate. There are historical allusions to Ralegh's part in the
colonization of Ireland; to the small Spanish-Catholic defence
force routed at Smerwick in 1580; and to John Aubrey's
description of Ralegh's amorous adventures:

> He loved a wench well; and one time getting up one of the
> Mayds of Honour up against a tree in a Wood ('twas his first
> Lady) who seemed at first boarding to be something fearfull
> of her Honour, and modest, she cryed, sweet Sir Walter,
> what doe you me ask; Will you undoe me? Nay, sweet Sir
> Walter! Sweet Sir Walter! Sir Walter! At last as the danger
> and the pleasure at the same time grew higher, she cryed in
> the extasey, Swisser, Swatter, Swisser, Swatter. She proved
> with child, and I doubt not but this Hero tooke care of them
> both, as also that the Product was more than an ordinary
> mortal.[52]

On another level the poem describes a linguistic and literary
conquest, Ralegh's 'broad Devonshire' (the phrase is again
Aubrey's) overcoming the 'Irish' of the ruined maid, 'Iambic
drums / Of English' beating through the woods that used
to harbour those Gaelic poets of the 'Hidden Ireland' once
celebrated by Daniel Corkery. Meanwhile Ralegh's 'superb
crest' (boat-prow, penis, heraldic emblem) 'drives inland': the
Irish maid is exploited for temporary pleasure, but all the while

65

Ralegh's real loyalties lie at home with Queen Elizabeth.

The geographical image here – 'Ireland is backed to England' – is picked up again in 'Act of Union', in which the two countries are pictured as a man and woman lying together, England the 'tall kingdom', 'imperially male', lying over the shoulder of Ireland. This poem first appeared in *The Listener* in February 1973 as four sonnets under the title 'A New Life'; revising it for *North*, where it runs to only half the length of the original, Heaney put greater emphasis on the destructiveness of the union by dropping a final hopeful line about a 'triangle of forces solved in love' and by focusing greater attention on the 'child' of the union, the 'obstinate fifth column' of Ulster Protestants with their 'parasitical / And ignorant little fists'. If it is a measure of Heaney's growing pessimism about political solutions in the North that the poem changed course in this way, it is also a mark of his race and religion that he should lay the blame where he does.

*

In allowing their author's tribal prejudices as an Irish Catholic to show through, these last poems in Part I of *North* feed into the poems of Part II, where, as we move to the present day, resentments are more openly declared. There is a hostile caricature of a parading Orange drummer 'lodging thunder / Grossly there between his chin and his knees' (*N*, p. 68) (*grossly*, we note, where Catholic violence had been *exact*); there is the poem 'Freedman', in which the poet's anglicized education is compared to that of a slave's under the Romans ('I was under that thumb too like all my caste'; *N*, p. 61); and, however lightly worn, there is the fear of Royal Ulster Constabulary and British Army harassment which comes over in the reminiscences of 'The Ministry of Fear' and 'A Constable Calls' (the latter another poem revised for *North*: it first appeared in Padraic Fiacc's *The Wearing of the Black* anthology[53] as a prose-poem). Yet the overall tone of Part II is far from resentful or bitter. England may be imperialistic but is also, it appears, the provider of Wordsworth, Hopkins and a literary tradition in which Heaney aspires to participate ('Ulster was British, but with no rights on / The English lyric'; *N*, p. 65). Moreover, no matter where the loyalties of these poems lie, Heaney does not purport to offer an easy Republican or 'repartition' or 'Troops Out' solution to the Northern crisis. Describing 'bangs' of gunfire in Belfast he writes, in an aside,

> (It's tempting here to rhyme on 'labour pangs'
> And diagnose a rebirth in our plight
>
> But that would be to ignore other symptoms.) (*N*, p. 58)

The 'symptoms', of course, include not just the intransigence of Ian Paisley and the Ulster Protestants but the ancient impulse towards feud and violence which Heaney has explored in the poems of Part I of *North*. If the documentary reportage of 'Whatever You Say, Say Nothing' seems superficial in comparison to such poems – a 'clichéd condemnation of clichés', Edna Longley has called it[54] – then that is partly the point: Heaney seeks to convince us that the language of contemporary reporting about Northern Ireland ('backlash', 'crackdown', 'escalation', 'polarization') is, as he puts it, 'remote from the psychology of the Irishmen and Ulstermen who do the killing' (*P*, p. 57) in a way that an ancient language of votive offerings and territorial propitiations is not. In 'Kinship' Heaney addresses one of the first foreign correspondents in Ireland, the Tacitus of *Agricola* and *Germania*: carefully choosing the word 'report' he asks

> report us fairly,
> how we slaughter
> for the common good
>
> and shave the heads
> of the notorious,
> how the goddess swallows
> our love and terror. (*N*, p. 45)

I have spent many hours over these lines and come back to them many times. For that phrase 'slaughter for the common good' is reminiscent of, and in its own way as controversial as, Auden's phrase in 'Spain' about 'the necessary murder', a phrase that Auden changed after George Orwell had objected to it on the grounds that 'it could only be written by a person to whom murder is at most a word, . . . the kind of person who is always somewhere else when the trigger is pulled.'[55] Heaney, acute as always, takes on board such an accusation when he writes later in *North*, 'We tremble near the flames but want no truck / With the actual firing' (*N*, p. 58). But 'Kinship' itself embodies no such liberal conscience: like 'Punishment', it ends up speaking the language of the tribe, brutal though that language may be. And, if we cannot quite believe that Heaney really supposes slaughter such as the IRA carried out in Ireland and England in the 1970s to be 'for the common good', nor is there anything to suggest that the phrase is intended to be some kind of civilized irony – that would be to read into the poem a gap between the speaker and his subject which is simply not there. It is one of several points in *North* where one feels that Heaney is not writing his poems but having them written for him, his frieze composed almost in spite of him by the 'anonymities' of race and religion. And at such moments, like it or not, his poetry grants sectarian killing in Northern Ireland a historical respectability which it is not usually granted in day-to-day journalism: precedent becomes, if not a justification, then at least an 'explanation'.

North is in many ways a bleak book, and that bleakness comes less from the imagery of a blood-stained and 'skull-capped' ground than from the author's fatalism, his fear that even if we do understand the past we may still be condemned to repeat it. The titles of all Heaney's previous books had embodied some notion of progress: the naturalist might be dead but the poet would take his place; the door into the dark would open up new worlds; see the winter out and spring might not be far behind. But *North* is just north, an arctic cul-de-sac from which one can escape only by turning round and going south (which, as it happens, Heaney did). Conor Cruise O'Brien, in his review of *North*, described Heaney as being 'on intimate terms with doom' and compared *North* to a Kipling story in which 'bright and tender hopes are snuffed out by ineluctable destiny, the hand of Thor'.[56] That feeling of tragedy and destiny certainly comes over on many occasions during the book.

Yet *North* is more in the end than a book of darkness and gloom: for reasons difficult to explain, there is something comforting about it. Some would argue that it is precisely the feeling of tragic inevitability which makes it comforting, that contemporary events in Ulster become more bearable, perhaps even seem smaller in significance, when placed in the context of 2000 years' northern European experience. Heaney himself seems to toy with such an idea when he writes of 'how the goddess swallows / our love and terror', time bearing all away before it. But, if there is some comfort and catharsis in *North*, I prefer to think that it comes less from this than from Heaney's honesty, his exactness, his unwavering pursuit of a myth through which we might understand Northern Ireland today. For, though Heaney shares Auden's suspicion that 'poetry makes nothing happen', he also shares his belief that poetry may extend our knowledge of good and evil, bringing us to the point where it is possible to make a rational choice. 'I think a poet cannot influence events in the North', he has said, 'because it is the men of action that are influencing everybody and everything, but I do believe that poetry is its own special action and that having its own mode of consciousness, its own mode of reality, has its own efficacy gradually.'[57] *North* is Heaney's most concerted effort to interpret the tragic history of Ulster, and if the book demands a full look at the worst, and has its moments of defeat and determinism, there nevertheless persists in it the conviction that the structures of feeling may slowly be changed.

5

THE HEDGE-SCHOOL: 'FIELD WORK'

> The Muses love me: I shall throw
> My gloom and fears to the winds to blow
>   Over the Cretan seas
>   Anyhow they please,
>
> Happy to neither know nor care
> Which northern king beneath the Bear
>   From his frost-bitten shore
>   Threatens the world with war . . .
>   (Horace, *Odes*, Bk I (trans. James Michie))

Field Work (1979) begins not at the beginning but, as is Heaney's custom, with the last poem of the book that preceded it. 'Exposure' is exactly what its title implies – a confessional. Written from the dripping trees of Wicklow (southern, rural, away from the Troubles), it lets us in on its author's worryings over the seemingly incompatible demands of art and social concern. The two previous poems in *North* have shown him receiving conflicting advice about his poetic responsibilities: 'try to touch the people', one person urges ('Summer 1969'); 'Go your own way. / Do your own work,' says another ('Fosterage'). The conflict arises again here as the poet walks through the countryside. On the one hand are those who see poetry as a social instrument, a bludgeoning tool, 'a slingstone / Whirled for the desperate.' On the other are the friends whose 'Beautiful prismatic counselling' (a bit 'precious' and aesthete-like, the phrase makes them sound) would have him strive for the 'diamond absolutes', the beauty and permanence of the perfectly achieved work of art. These voices sound accusingly in the poet's head – even the rain seems to 'Mutter about let-downs and erosions' – and an air of wistfulness and defeat hangs over him. But in the end he rises to an almost manifesto-like self-definition:

> I am neither internee nor informer;
> An inner émigré, grown long-haired
> And thoughtful; a wood-kerne
>
> Escaped from the massacre,
> Taking protective colouring
> From bole and bark, feeling
> Every wind that blows;
>
> Who, blowing up these sparks
> For their meagre heat, have missed
> The once-in-a-lifetime portent,
> The comet's pulsing rose. (*N*, p. 73)

Those three semicolons, and the gap between the word 'Who' and its antecedent, lend the conclusion of this poem an air of ambiguity; but its drift is clear. The suggestion is that Heaney, having withdrawn into his art, 'long-haired / And thoughtful', has missed the opportunity to observe a unique historical moment in the North. But against that we have to consider what missing a 'once-in-a-lifetime portent' amounts to when weighed against the absolutes of art. The poem reaches no tidy resolution, but for all its tentativeness does seem to move towards a position of strength: irresolution but independence.

What 'Exposure' leaves us with, *Field Work* takes up and develops. Its jacket cover reproduces a section of a large-scale map showing the gate-lodge at Glanmore, County Wicklow, to which Heaney and his family came to live in July 1972, and where they stayed for four years before making their home in Dublin. The poetry in *Field Work* is deeply conscious of that move into the Republic and the countryside. Heaney, after all, had spent his first thirty-three years in the North, nearly half of them in the city of Belfast, and by 1972 was a public, spokes-man-like figure and celebrity there. He also had a teaching job at the Queen's University which he enjoyed. Although the decision to leave Belfast was on one level practical and straight-forward (he wanted to devote himself full-time to writing, and the offer of the use of a cottage belonging to a Canadian friend, Ann Saddlemeyer, was a chance to break old rhythms and routines), it had many reverberations. He himself described it as 'emblematic' and as having a 'political dimension',[58] and certainly the press saw it in this way: one Eire newspaper ran the headline 'ULSTER POET MOVES SOUTH', while in Belfast *The Protestant Telegraph* devoted a half-page to the move, iden-tifying Heaney as 'the well-known Papish propagandist'.[59] In such circumstances it was not surprising that the move should have been seen by some as a betrayal of the Northern Catholic community and should have aroused in Heaney feelings of unease and even guilt.

One important consequence was the new seriousness he brought to his thinking about the writer and his responsibili-ties. As he put it: 'Those four years were an important growth time when I was asking myself questions about the proper function of poets and poetry and learning a new commitment to the art.'[60] *Field Work* is indeed Heaney's most questioning book, one that returns many times to the issues raised in 'Exposure', and one in which the poet is to be found anxiously consulting friends, relations, sibyls, but above all himself: 'Who's sorry for our trouble?', 'What will become of us?', 'What do we say any more / to conjure the salt of our earth?', 'how culpable was he / that last night . . . ?', 'How perilous is it to choose / not to love the life we're shown?', 'What is my apology for poetry?', 'Whose is the life / Most dedicated and exemplary?', and so on. There are no easy answers, but there is a drift towards placing art above all else — the 'diamond absolutes' are decisively preferred to the 'slingstone / Whirled for the desperate'. Heaney's reviews from the mid-1970s bear this development out, suggesting a reaction against the kind of political pressure he had been under in Belfast and to which *North* had been a response. In a review of 1975 he can be found complaining that 'internment and the North have become a spectator sport' (*P*, p. 214), and a 1974 account of Mandel-stam's relationship with the Russian government claims: 'We live here in critical times ourselves, when the idea of poetry as an art is in danger of being overshadowed by a quest for poetry as a diagram of political attitudes. Some commentators have all the fussy literalism of an official from the ministry of truth' (*P*, pp. 219–20).

It is in response to such attitudes that Heaney offers his 'field work'. Teasingly confronting what he calls the 'simple-minded' belief that 'poems with rural or archaic images . . . aren't engaging with the modern world',[61] he places at the centre of the collection ten highly wrought sonnets about the experience of living in Glanmore, with its mists and wet hedges, its ploughs and tractors, its cuckoos and corncrakes, its rats and deer, its rowans and elderberries, and so on. The subtext is Heaney's sense of himself as resembling other famous figures who retreated into the sanctuary of rural life: Horace, in his 'leafy privacy' far from Rome (Ann Saddle-meyer's loan of the Wicklow gate-lodge is like Maecenas' gift of the Sabine farm); Virgil, whose *Georgics* gave instruc-tions in agriculture; Sweeney, of the Irish epic poem, who after the noise of battle was turned into a bird and roamed the countryside. *Field Work* is conscious of appearing to be a similar withdrawal: the topography is much more restricted than that of *North* (ordnance-survey scale), the time-scale drastically diminished (four years rather than 2000), the tone quietly reverential, the subject-matter and poetic line a return to the first two books. 'Now the good life could be to cross a field / And art a paradigm of earth new from the lathe / Of ploughs' (*FW*, p. 33), he writes in the first of these sonnets, knowing full well the taunt he is offering to 'the world of illiterates and politicians' (*P*, p. 100). The second sonnet, too, self-consciously dramatizes a 'turning-point' in his career, bringing visually alive that tired critical phrase:

Then I landed in the hedge-school of Glanmore

And from the backs of ditches hoped to raise
A voice caught back off slug-horn and slow chanter
That might continue, hold, dispel, appease:
Vowels ploughed into other, opened ground,
Each verse returning like the plough turned round.

(*FW*, p. 34)

There is a certain amount of twinkling-eyed irony in that first
line. For hedge-schools, as Heaney's friend Brian Friel reminds
us in his play *Translations* (1980), were the schools operated
by and for Irish Catholic peasants at a time when no official
provision for their education existed. Based in barns, cowsheds
and even the open air, hedge-schools survived until the introduction of state education in 1831, and were the reason why
some Irish peasants had such a remarkable knowledge of the
classics. The Glanmore hedge-school is not, then, to be con-
fused with the Georgian nature-school: Heaney's pun on the
word implies that he has been getting for himself a grass-roots
education – 'radical' in the original sense of that word. *Field
Work* is not, in other words, quite the regression it plays at
being: the search for a voice that 'might continue, hold, dispel,
appease' has not been abandoned but rather shifted to new
ground.

   One feature of this shift is the emphasis now placed on the
notion of 'trust': trust between poet and reader, poet and
subject-matter, but above all between poet and language.
Christopher Ricks rightly makes much of the trust in *Field
Work*, suggesting that the book 'could have been created only
by an experienced poet secure in the grounded trust that he is
trusted. Heaney is the most trusted poet of our islands.'[62]
'Trust', however, is a word that Heaney had not used since his
'Honeymoon Flight' in *Death of a Naturalist*, which compared
the descent of an aircraft to the beginning of a marriage:
'Travellers, at this point, can only trust.' That trust in trust now
returns – or tries to – with the opening poem of *Field Work*,
'Oysters', where the travellers are the poet and some compan-

ions who have driven to the coast and are 'toasting friendship' with a meal of oysters. The oysters have the sense of an emblem, stirring as so often before the poet's historical and political conscience. 'Split', 'violated', 'ripped and shucked and scattered', they threaten to become another of his symbols of ancient barbarism. A harmless platter of them acquires all the harm of an imperialist plunder:

> Over the Alps, packed deep in hay and snow,
> The Romans hauled their oysters south to Rome:
> I saw damp panniers disgorge
> The frond-lipped, brine-stung
> Glut of privilege
>
> And was angry that my trust could not repose
> In the clear light, like poetry or freedom
> Leaning in from sea. I ate the day
> Deliberately, that its tang
> Might quicken me all into verb, pure verb. (*FW*, p. 11)

The final stanza breaks not just with the four that precede it but with the hardened customs of several years. History, as so often before, unloads its foul lumber, blundering in on the pleasures of the meal and the text: how is the poet to gorge himself when the past disgorges all this? But now, as never before, Heaney is angry with himself for allowing the intrusion. He aspires to a poetry of 'clear light', untrammelled by the darkness and opacity of the past. To eat the day is to give oneself up to the present; being 'verb, pure verb', liberated from names and nouns and qualifiers, becomes an image of artistic independence. For while the sentence is a miniature social order, requiring strict and responsible behaviour of its constituents, the 'pure verb' (on its own, and unsullied) acts as it chooses. In this opening poem Heaney announces his determination to be determined by history no longer: his mind darting freely wherever it will, he will be leant on only by the poetic imagination.

*

That the imagination may nevertheless continue to tax him with the matter of the North and its Troubles, the next group of poems in *Field Work* makes clear. 'After a Killing' (the first of 'Triptych') was written after the murder of the British Ambassador to Ireland, Christopher Ewart-Biggs, in July 1976. The 'march at Newry' in 'At the Water's Edge' (the last of 'Triptych') took place in March 1972, in protest against the thirteen killings on Bloody Sunday, 30 January 1972. 'The Strand at Lough Beg' is in memory of Colum McCartney, a cousin of Heaney's shot dead one night while driving home in County Armagh ('The red lamp swung, the sudden brakes and stalling / Engine, voices, heads hooded and the cold-nosed gun'; *FW*, p. 17). 'A Postcard from North Antrim' is an elegy for Sean Armstrong, a social worker and friend of Heaney's from his days at Queen's, whose 'candid forehead stopped / A point-blank teatime bullet' (*FW*, p. 19). 'Casualty' was written for a man called Louis O'Neill, who frequented the pub run by Heaney's father-in-law and was blown up the Wednesday after Bloody Sunday. There is also 'The Toome Road', which describes the poet's early-morning encounter with a convoy of British Army vehicles. Once again we find him asking a question – though less from bafflement here than from indignation:

> How long were they approaching down my roads
> As if they owned them? The whole country was sleeping.
> I had rights-of-way, fields, cattle in my keeping,
> Tractors hitched to buckrakes in open sheds,
> Silos, chill gates, wet slates, the greens and reds
> Of outhouse roofs. Whom should I run to tell . . . ?
>
> (*FW*, p. 15)

These lines are perhaps intended to recall Patrick Kavanagh's similarly proprietorial 'I am king / Of banks and stones and every blooming thing' (which Heaney quotes in *Preoccupations*, p. 117), for Kavanagh, too, well understood Northern sensitivity on the matter of 'rights-of-way'. That expression, which turns up many times in Heaney's poetry, refers here to no farmer's feud but to a racial and political confrontation – Heaney speaks in the tones of a native whose territory has been invaded. The poem ends defiantly by referring to the 'untoppled omphalos': this is both the water-pump described in his memories of 'Mossbawn' – '*omphalos, omphalos, omphalos* . . . its blunt and falling music becomes the music of somebody pumping water at the pump outside our back door' (*P*, p. 17; see also *S*, p. 8) – and the poet's immutable tribal loyalties.

Heaney does not, then, leave Ulster behind him while living in Wicklow, any more than he left Derry behind him while living in Belfast. But his tone is now elegiac, concerned not to probe the causes of a nation's sorrow but to mourn the loss of relatives and friends. There are, in fact, no fewer than six elegies in the book, three to victims of the Troubles and three to fellow artists (Robert Lowell, Francis Ledwidge, Sean O'Riada). In 'The Guttural Muse' Heaney writes of 'the slimy tench / Once called the "doctor fish" because his slime / Was said to heal the wounds of fish that touched it' (*FW*, p. 28). Heaney might still like to be that tench, as he thought he was in *Wintering Out* and *North*, a helper and healer. But he confesses to feeling 'like some old pike all badged with sores', and becomes instead an embalmer or anointer, his gifts offered to the dead rather than the living, his task to provide fitting burials rather than to think of means to prevent them. It is as an anointer of his dead cousin that he appears, movingly, in 'The Strand at Lough Beg', where we see him kneel like Virgil wiping Dante's face with rushes and dew in *Purgatorio*:

> I dab you clean with moss
> Fine as the drizzle out of a low cloud.
> I lift you under the arms and lay you flat.
> With rushes that shoot green again, I plait
> Green scapulars to wear over your shroud. (*FW*, p. 18)

In *North* Heaney had resurrected the dead, raising the Bog People out of the past. His one effort to perform similar miracles here – 'Get up from your blood on the floor', he orders

Sean Armstrong (*FW*, p. 20) – is poignant in its hope against hope.

The changed role Heaney envisages for himself is most fully explored in 'Casualty'. This poem considers the implications of one of the most haunting deaths of the Troubles – that of an acquaintance who, defying the curfew imposed by Catholics in mourning for the thirteen men shot dead by British para-troopers on Bloody Sunday, was 'blown to bits' while out for his customary evening's drinking: the bomb had been planted by his own people. When, in 'Punishment', Heaney had con-sidered similar tribal justice – the putting to death of an adul-teress, the tarring and feathering of disloyal Catholic girls – his sympathies were balanced between pity for the victims and understanding of the tribe's 'exact' revenge, tipping finally towards the latter. Here there is the same impression of earnest reflection on a difficult moral problem: 'How culpable was he', Heaney asks, 'That last night when he broke / Our tribe's complicity?' (*FW*, p. 23). Here, however, the imagery works to exculpate the dead man. A fisherman by day, he 'drank like a fish / Nightly, naturally / Swimming towards the lure / Of warm lit-up places' (*FW*, p. 23). *Naturally*: as the word 'connive' swung Heaney one way in 'Punishment', so that word 'natur-ally' swings him the opposite way here, insisting that the man could no more help but be individualistic than can a fish help being obedient to its own rhythms. A loner by instinct (we learn of the fisherman's shyness and slyness, his preference of a 'discreet dumb-show' to speech), he has none of the 'shoaling' habits that would have enabled him to conform. Thus far Heaney excuses the man; but in the last section of the poem he goes further, celebrating his independence as a paradigm of artistic activity:

> To get out early, haul
> Steadily off the bottom,
> Dispraise the catch, and smile
> As you find a rhythm
> Working you, slow mile by mile,

>   Into your proper haunt
>   Somewhere, well out, beyond . . . (*FW*, p. 24)

If we were in danger of missing here Heaney's idea of poetry as being a kind of 'catch' from the bottom of the psyche, the words 'working' and 'rhythm' leave us in no doubt of the intended analogy. The thinking is of a traditional Romantic kind, the poet seen as someone whose pursuit of art places him above and beyond the demands of the tribe. And the governing spirits of the poem are not Northern poets like Kavanagh and Montague but those peremptory Southerners Joyce and Yeats: the Joyce who recognized the need of the artist to fly free of the nets of nationality, language and religion; and the Yeats whose poem 'The Fisherman' was written in the same two-to-three-stress line as 'Casualty', looks to the same kind of 'wise and simple man' for moral and poetic instruction, and marks the same kind of turning away from populist ambitions to a poetry that will be 'maybe as cold / and passionate as the dawn'. Heaney's is (as he says in 'Casualty') a 'tentative art', shyer and less expostulating, more reluctant than was the poetry of his predecessors to express contempt for the community as a sow eating its farrow or a 'fool-driven land'. But he comes noticeably closer to rejecting its values here than ever before. He speaks of its 'complicity', the word implying not just confederacy but 'partnership in an evil action' (*OED*), and his image of the funeral for the victims of Bloody Sunday –

>   The common funeral
>   Unrolled its swaddling band,
>   Lapping, tightening
>   Till we were braced and bound
>   Like brothers in a ring (*FW*, p. 22)

– has a sense of constriction and suffocation as well as of communion: 'swaddling band', benign sounding when applied to new babies, here suggests the oppressiveness of the *Lumpenproletariat* ('swad' used to mean 'mass' or 'clump', and 'swaddish' means 'loutish'); and 'braced' and 'bound' are similarly

79

destructive of the perfect commonalty that might have been suggested by the image of the ring. The tribe here begins to seem a threat to independence. Two earlier draft versions of 'Casualty' had put the matter more blatantly, one describing the observers of the curfew as 'wiser hypocrites', the other ending up:

> Sometimes men obtain
> A power when they betray
> And swim out from the shoal,
> Daring to make free.[63]

Heaney's cancellation of these lines suggests that he is still tugged by old currents of feeling; and it is a mark of his tentative art, his desire to make soundings rather than to be resounding, that the final version ends with his continuing to cast about ('Question me again,' he asks the fisherman) rather than with a catch. Nevertheless it is hard to mistake the direction in which the poem is moving, and hard not to believe that in the fisherman's alienation from his people – 'he would not be held / At home by his own crowd' (*FW*, p. 22) – Heaney happened on an emblem for his own move to Glanmore.

The image of the circle used in 'Casualty' recurs throughout *Field Work*, acting as the linchpin of an argument about art and social responsibility. On the one hand, the circle symbolizes artistic perfection, such as is to be found in the 'Glanmore Sonnets', where every last line completes themes taken up in the first, 'each verse returning like the plough turned round', or in 'The Harvest Bow', whose 'golden loops' provide access from the material world into a spiritual one, 'gleaning the unsaid off the palpable'. On the other hand, circles symbolize domestic and marital perfection, as we find in the 'Field Work' sequence, where there are a number of circular motifs – eyes, coins, rings, moons, sunflowers, vaccination marks. Between these two fulfilling possibilities are less positive ones: circles can symbolize artistic self-enclosure, and poets who pursue artistic perfection to the neglect of their family and tribe are likely to find themselves being wished to hell – as Heaney is, amusingly, in 'An Afterwards', where his long-suffering wife is described as wanting to 'plunge all poets in the ninth circle' and reprovingly demands of him

Why could you not have, oftener, in our years

Unclenched, and come down laughing from your room
And walked the twilight with me and your children . . . ?
(*FW*, p. 44)

Artistic endeavour takes its toll, excluding even the poet's intimates from its charmed circle. So too those who allow the clenched circles of art to be broken by the clenched fists of politics are equally punishable by damnation. In the excellent 'Leavings' this is the fate of that desecrator Thomas Cromwell, who was responsible as Henry VIII's Chief Minister for the dissolution of the monasteries, 'the sweet tenor latin / forever banished, / the sumptuous windows / threshed clear' (*FW*, p. 57); 'Which circle does he tread?' for his sins Heaney wonders, again referring to Dante.

Dante's are the most infernal circles of all, and recur at several points in *Field Work*, which concludes with a translation of cantos XXXII and XXXIII of the *Inferno*. The presence of Dante's circles reflects a new emphasis on moral responsibility, an emphasis quite antithetical to the determinism of *North*. 'The way we are living, / timorous or bold, / will have been our life' (*FW*, p. 31), the 'Elegy' to Robert Lowell dauntingly begins: ancestry and environment will not suffice to explain our actions; we exercise free choice and are judged accordingly. Heaney's Catholicism, more a matter of local political alignments in his earlier work, here assumes a sterner, explicitly religious dimension. Voices are raised in judgement and warning – 'Unless forgiveness finds its nerve', '*Remember the Giver*', 'the sins / Of Ugolino, who betrayed your forts, / Should never have been visited on his sons'. But if Dante's influence is discernible in the tones of *Field Work*, it does not make the book merely bleakly admonitory. Reading *The Divine Com-*

edy, Heaney has said, 'is to go through a refining element, to be steadied and reminded of the possible dimensions of life',[64] and his poems too strive to achieve such steadying reminders – moments of grace that block out the island's 'comfortless noises'. One such moment comes in 'After a Killing', where suddenly, miraculously, 'the heart lifts' because of the simple, restorative appearance of a girl who arrives like Ceres

> Carrying a basket full of new potatoes,
> Three tight green cabbages, and carrots
> With the tops and mould still fresh on them. (*FW*, p. 12)

In another poem from this same 'Triptych' Heaney describes himself wanting 'to bow down, to offer up', and this posture, too, is a characteristic of *Field Work*: as well as the 'masculine rectitude of the Ten Commandments' we have the 'feminine' humility of a Marian religion, which genuflectingly murmurs its devotion to the things of this world[65] – whether a rowan 'like a lipsticked girl' or the 'slow diminuendo' of a filling bucket. Naming things, as Patrick Kavanagh once said in his poem about a hospital ward, is a sort of religious ceremony, 'the love-act and its pledge'; and Heaney loves to name names, reminding us that to 'list' once meant not just to document but to love or desire: 'When they said *Carrickfergus* I could hear / the frosty echo of saltminers' picks' (*FW*, p. 27); 'Elderberry? It is shires dreaming wine' (*FW*, p. 37); 'Pisa! Pisa, your sounds are like a hiss / Sizzling in our country's grassy language' (*FW*, p. 63).

This Marian reverence for names and objects underlies the success of the love poems (or more properly marriage poems) in *Field Work*, the first ones in Heaney's *œuvre* to carry an authenticity of feeling. His previous efforts to write to and about his wife had foundered, lapsing into Movement mannerism in *Death of a Naturalist* and high-pitched Plath-like confessionalism in *Wintering Out*. Here he discovers that it is through an obsessive objectifying that he can best be subjective, and through a relentless zoomorphosizing that he can be most tenderly human. Scarcely womanly at all, the poet's wife appears as an otter, a skunk, a sand-martin's nest, and a piece of low-lying land reclaimed from the sea. Though equations of one's lover with natural phenomena are older than even Burns's red, red rose, Heaney takes great risks in choosing such unromantic analogies and in making so much of humdrum blemishes like 'the vaccination mark / stretched on your upper arm' (*FW*, p. 52). But if his wife is 'stained', she is 'stained to perfection' (as woodstaining enriches the look of wood), and the poems triumphantly justify their chancy procedures by achieving a blend of sexual passion and domestic affection unique in modern British poetry – not, though, unique in American, Robert Lowell's Lizzie and Harriet poems having been a useful model for Heaney. In 'The Skunk' (a very Lowell-like title and poem) the highly erotic 'sootfall of your things at bedtime' (the clothes slip as silkily to the ground as do those of Thomas Wyatt's lover 'when her loose gown did from her shoulders fall') passes to the maritally routine: 'Your head-down, tail-up hunt in a bottom drawer / For the black plunge-line nightdress' (*FW*, p. 48). That 'the' in the last line spells husbandly familiarity, not sensual arousal, but the poem sacrifices neither unity of tone nor strong feeling.

*

The poet's wife is also an important presence in the 'Glanmore Sonnets', the central sequence of *Field Work* (it is placed exactly midway through the book), which draws together the themes of art, love, language and responsibility to be found elsewhere through the collection. The sequence marks Heaney's return not just to the countryside but to the mainstream of English poetry: having begun in imitation of Ted Hughes and then looked more to his own countrymen, he now takes his place in an English lyric tradition that includes Wyatt at one end and Wordsworth at the other. Both these writers are indeed alluded to. Wyatt's 'They flee from me . . .', hinted at in 'The Skunk', is explicitly drawn on in the dream related in the last Glanmore sonnet (*FW*, p. 42), contributing to the poem's erotic memory of the 'covenants of flesh':

> And in that dream I dreamt – how like you this? –
> Our first night years ago in that hotel
> When you came with your deliberate kiss . . . (Heaney)

> She caught me in her arms long and small
> There with all sweetly did me kiss
> And softly said *dear heart, how like you this?* (Wyatt)

Wordsworth appears at the beginning of the sequence, referred to nervously in Sonnet III, where the poet brings up '". . . Dorothy and William –" She interrupts: / "You're not going to compare us two . . . ?"' (*FW*, p. 35), and lying behind the image of the poet-as-ploughman in the first two sonnets, as a parallel *Preoccupations* passage on Wordsworth's methods of composition makes clear:

> The continuity of the things was what was important, the onward inward pouring out, up and down the gravel path, the crunch and scuffle of the gravel working like a metre or a metronome under the rhythms of the ongoing chaunt, those 'trances of thought and mountings of the mind' somehow aided by the automatic, monotonous turns and returns of the walk. . . . The poet as ploughman, if you like, and the suggestive etymology of the word 'verse' itself is pertinent in this context. 'Verse' comes from the Latin *versus* which could mean a line of poetry but could also mean the turn that a ploughman made at the head of the field as he finished one furrow and faced back into another. (*P*, p. 65)

In Sonnet II this becomes:

> Sensings, mountings from the hiding places,
> Words entering almost the sense of touch. . . .
> Vowels ploughed into other, opened ground,
> Each verse returning like the plough turned round.
>
> (*FW*, p. 34)

The poem and the essay make clear the extent to which Heaney shares with Wordsworth a notion of poetry as the opening up of the 'hiding places' of one's power, as a matter of 'sensings' and 'mountings'. (How characteristic of Heaney, but how like Wordsworth too, those plural participles are: *sensings, mountings, homecomings, leavings, makings, soundings*.) Throughout the 'Glanmore Sonnets' Heaney takes a Wordsworthian delight in the intimate, creative relationship between poetry and nature: the evening is 'crepuscular and iambic'; a breeze 'is cadences'; raindrops are 'lush with omen'; the poet himself is an 'etymologist of roots and graftings'. It is this evocation of harmony between land and language which gives the sequence, which has no obvious surface unity, an underlying force and direction.

In a review of an anthology of pastoral verse, Heaney admits that he has acquired the habit of talking 'of the countryside where we live in Wicklow as being pastoral rather than rural, trying to impose notions of a beautified landscape on the word in order to keep "rural" for the unselfconscious face of raggle-taggle farmland' (*P*, p. 173). The 'Glanmore Sonnets' are self-consciously pastoral right down to their 'classical' bay-tree and echoes of Horace and Virgil. Yet the sequence is not, as pastoral verse nowadays tends to be accused of being, either simplistic or escapist. Knottily textured, difficult, lush with omen, it does not merely happen on its pleasures and harmonies but has to wrest them from fragmentation and disorder. Beyond the images of delicate beauty – small ripples across water and heart, a 'rustling and twig-combing breeze', 'fuchsia in a drizzling noon' – lies the constant risk of intrusion and disillusion: 'distant gargling tractors', clanking trains, a rat that 'sways on the briar like infected fruit'. Ringed round by dangers, the poet and his wife succeed in making small epiphanic clearings. In Sonnet VII, for example the gales warned of on the midnight shipping forecast give way next morning to the poet's triumphant witnessing and saying aloud of 'A haven':

L'Etoile, Le Guillemot, La Belle Hélène
Nursed their bright names this morning in the bay
That toiled like mortar. It was marvellous
And actual, I said out loud, 'A haven,'
The word deepening, clearing, like the sky
Elsewhere on Minches, Cromarty, The Faroes. *(FW,* p. 39)

But we are made to understand that such look-we-have-come-throughs are temporary and precarious: as the epilogue to the 'Glanmore Sonnets', 'September Song', puts it, 'We toe the line / between the tree in leaf and the bare tree' *(FW,* p. 43). Heaney's characterization of himself and his wife, in the final sonnet, as 'Lorenzo and Jessica in a cold climate. / Diarmuid and Grainne waiting to be found' *(FW,* p. 42) adds to this feeling of vulnerability. Both these couples, the first Shakespearean, the second from Celtic myth, fled their homes in order to be together, living in constant danger of discovery and death. Even the final image of the sequence has its chilly undertow: it is not 'rest' which is seen on the couple's 'dewy dreaming faces' but 'respite', a parenthesis rather than a new chapter, the peace that comes not after but between. Thus, when Heaney writes, in 'The Harvest Bow', *'The end of art is peace* / Could be the motto of this frail device' *(FW,* p. 58), it is the qualification of 'frail' and 'could' that we notice as much as the italicized affirmation. Peace of one sort or another (his own, his readers', his nation's; psychological, civil and aesthetic) is what all his poetry works towards; and the 'Glanmore Sonnets' and *Field Work* come close to attaining peace. But he is too modest, or not confident enough, to want to press the claim: the hedge-school is also the school of hedging.

In many ways the 'Glanmore Sonnets' bring Seamus Heaney's poetic development full circle. It was with the silence of his ancestors that he began and it is a similar silence – 'a deep no sound', a 'dark hush' – that pervades this sonnet sequence.

In the meantime, however, he has resolved the tensions which characterized his early work: the formal, measured voice which he once awkwardly struggled to acquire is here achieved without strain; the troubling dichotomy of the 'explicit' and 'intuitive' in his work disappears; and the forms used are traditional ones that now at last embody his distinctive talent. It would be over-neat to make too much of this progression and return: *Field Work* is only the most recent phase in what one hopes will be a long career. But at the level of poetic language it is a crucial collection. In one of the 'Glanmore Sonnets' Heaney refers to 'the unsayable lights', implying that there exists a special zone into which language (both his and that of other poets) has been unable to penetrate. But *Field Work* promises that those 'lights' may become sayable after all because of Heaney's willingness to trust and treasure language, to cede to its authority, to allow himself to be nourished by its deep structures.

This trusting and treasuring not only makes Heaney a far stronger poet in his later work but has had important consequences for British poetry generally, encouraging a new generation of poets to turn to language itself as a source for poetry and helping bring about a new imaginative freedom and linguistic daring. I mean by that not that other poets have directly imitated him (though there has been an increased volume of sentimental poems about craftsmen and the joys of the countryside, a development for which his early poetry must be held partly responsible), but that he has been the key figure in a movement away from the Movement – he more than anyone has shown that it is possible to preserve the decencies and civilities of post-1945 British verse while breaking with the rationalistic mode that hampered it for so long. In this Heaney has had his final revenge on those who like to present him as an archaic outsider. Shaped in complex and surprising ways by his culture, he has in turn begun to shape the course of poetry in Britain today.

NOTES

1 A. Alvarez, 'A Fine Way with the Language', *New York Review of Books*, 6 March 1980, pp. 16–17.

2 His Radio Telefís Eireann broadcast of 1978, 'The God in the Tree', originally began with Saussure's distinction between *langue* and *parole*, though this does not appear in the printed version in *P*, p. 181.

3 Heaney, interview, in Monie Begley, *Rambles in Ireland* (Old Greenwich, Conn.: Devin-Adair, 1977), p. 164.

4 Anon., 'Life in Numbers', *The Times Literary Supplement*, 9 June 1966, p. 512.

5 Anon., 'Fear in a Tinful of Bait', *The Times Literary Supplement*, 17 July 1969, p. 770.

6 C. B. Cox, 'The Painter's Eye', *Spectator*, 20 May 1966, p. 638.

7 'An Interview with Seamus Heaney' (James Randall), *Ploughshares*, 5, 3 (1979), p. 14.

8 Heaney, interview, 'Le Clivage traditionnel', *Les Lettres nouvelles* (March 1973), p. 188.

9 Heaney, interview, in John Haffenden, *Viewpoints* (London: Faber, 1981), p. 63.

10 The poem was privately printed (Farnham, Surrey: Sceptre Press, 1970).

11 Heaney, 'John Bull's Other Island', *The Listener*, 29 September 1977, pp. 397–9.

12 A report in the *Daily Telegraph* of 20 July 1976 described how the setting of this poem as an O-level text had 'brought protests from parents on grounds of both content and the poem's earthy language. The poem ... was described by Mr Eldon Griffiths, Conservative MP for Bury St Edmunds, as "sick". Written by Sean Heany [*sic*] ... it begins "I was six when I first saw kittens

drown", and goes on to describe their death in language not encouraged in most homes.'

13 Quoted by Edna Longley, 'Stars and Horses, Pigs and Trees', *The Crane Bag*, 3, 2 (1979), p. 54.

14 E. Estyn Evans, *Irish Folk Ways* (London: Routledge, 1957), p. xv.

15 For further discussion of the Heaney–Evans connection, see John Wilson Foster, 'The Poetry of Seamus Heaney', *Critical Quarterly*, 16, 1 (Spring 1974), pp. 36–40.

16 Heaney, 'Frogman', *The Listener*, 4 July 1968, p. 11. The poem reads very much like a fleshing out of Patrick Kavanagh's remark that 'a man dabbles in verses and finds they are his life' (quoted by Heaney in *P*, p. 34).

17 A. T. Q. Stewart, *The Narrow Ground: Aspects of Ulster 1609–1969* (London: Faber, 1977), pp. 181–2.

18 Edward Pygge, *The Review*, 22 (June 1970), p. 62.

19 Christopher Ricks, 'Lasting Things', *The Listener*, 26 June 1969, p. 900.

20 Quoted in Terence Brown, *Northern Voices: Poets from Ulster* (Dublin: Gill and Macmillan, 1975), p. 81.

21 Quoted in ibid., p. 219.

22 Heaney, 'Celtic Fringe, Viking Fringe', *The Listener*, 21 August 1969, p. 255.

23 Heaney, interview, 'Unhappy and at Home' (Seamus Deane), *The Crane Bag*, 1, 1 (1977), p. 61.

24 Seamus Deane, in Douglas Dunn (ed.), *Two Decades of Irish Writing* (Manchester: Carcanet, 1975), p. 8.

25 Heaney, 'Old Derry's Walls', *The Listener*, 24 October 1968, p. 522. The earlier article was 'Out of London: Ulster's Troubles', *New Statesman*, 1 July 1966, pp. 23–4.

26 Quoted in Karl Miller, 'Opinion', *The Review*, 27–8 (Autumn–Winter 1971–2), pp. 47–8.

27 Heaney, *Rambles in Ireland* interview, p. 165.

28 Heaney, 'The Saturday Interview' (Caroline Walsh), *Irish Times*, 6 December 1975, p. 5.

29 P. L. Henry, in G. B. Adams and others, *Ulster Dialects: An Introductory Symposium* (Holywood: Ulster Folk Museum, 1964), p. 147.

30 See Heaney, 'King of the Dark', *The Listener*, 5 February 1970, p. 182.

31 See Anne Ross, *Pagan Celtic Britain* (London: Routledge, 1967), p. 84, fig. 51.

32 Estyn Evans, op. cit., pp. 185, 196–8.

33 Heaney, 'Summoning Lazarus', *The Listener*, 6 June 1974, pp. 741–2.
34 See P. V. Glob, *The Bog People* (London: Faber, 1969).
35 Heaney, *The Crane Bag* interview, p. 65.
36 Heaney, *Viewpoints* interview, p. 68.
37 Heaney, *Rambles in Ireland* interview, p. 162.
38 *The Tain*, ed. and trans. Thomas Kinsella (London and Dublin: Oxford University Press/Dolmen, 1970).
39 John Montague, *The Rough Field* (Dublin: Dolmen, 1973).
40 Heaney, *The Crane Bag* interview, p. 65.
41 Ibid., p. 66.
42 Heaney, interview (Harriet Cooke), *Irish Times*, 28 December 1973, p. 8.
43 Anthony Thwaite, 'Neighbourly Murders', *The Times Literary Supplement*, 1 August 1975, p. 866.
44 Martin Dodsworth, 'New Poetry', *The Guardian*, 12 June 1975, p. 9.
45 Ciaran Carson, 'Escaped from the Massacre?', *The Honest Ulsterman*, 50 (Winter 1975), p. 186.
46 Heaney, *Poetry Book Society Bulletin*, 85 (Summer 1975), p. 1.
47 Heaney, *Rambles in Ireland* interview, p. 169.
48 Heaney himself explains the poem in this way in both the *Crane Bag* interview, p. 63, and the *Viewpoints* interview, pp. 69–70.
49 Heaney, *Ploughshares* interview, pp. 19–20.
50 Heaney, 'Mother Ireland', *The Listener*, 7 December 1972, p. 790.
51 Heaney, 'Delirium of the Brave', *The Listener*, 27 November 1969, p. 759.
52 John Aubrey, *Brief Lives* (Harmondsworth: Penguin, 1972), p. 418.
53 Padraic Fiacc (ed.), *The Wearing of the Black: Contemporary Ulster Poetry* (Belfast: Blackstaff, 1974).
54 Edna Longley, 'Fire and Air', *The Honest Ulsterman*, 50 (Winter 1975), p. 182.
55 George Orwell, 'Inside the Whale', *Collected Essays, Journalism and Letters*, Vol. 1: *1920–1940* (Harmondsworth: Penguin, 1970), p. 566.
56 Conor Cruise O'Brien, 'A Slow North-East Wind', *The Listener*, 25 September 1975, p. 405.
57 Heaney, *Irish Times* (1975) interview, p. 5.
58 Heaney, in Edward Broadbridge (ed.), *Seamus Heaney* (Copenhagen: Danmarks Radio, 1977), p. 48, and in the *Ploughshares* interview, p. 8.

59 See Anthony Bailey, 'A Gift for Being in Touch', *Quest* (January–February 1978), p. 44.

60 Heaney, *Poetry Book Society Bulletin*, 102 (Autumn 1979), p. 1.

61 Heaney, *Viewpoints* interview, p. 66.

62 Christopher Ricks, 'The Mouth, the Meal and the Book', *London Review of Books*, 8 November 1979, p. 4.

63 Heaney showed these two draft versions to a postgraduate seminar at University College, London, in 1977.

64 Heaney, 'Treely and Rurally', *Quarto*, 9 (August 1980), p. 14.

65 Heaney's distinction between these two kinds of religious impulse can be found in the *Viewpoints* interview, pp. 60–1.

BIBLIOGRAPHY

WORKS BY SEAMUS HEANEY

Books and pamphlets

Full-length collections are indicated by an asterisk (*).

Eleven Poems. Belfast: Festival Publications, Queen's University, 1965.

*Death of a Naturalist.** London: Faber, 1966. New York: Oxford University Press, 1966.

A Lough Neagh Sequence. Manchester: Phoenix Pamphlet Poets, 1969.

*Door into the Dark.** London: Faber, 1969. New York: Oxford University Press, 1969.

*Wintering Out.** London: Faber, 1972. New York: Oxford University Press, 1972.

Soundings. Belfast: Blackstaff, 1972.

Stations. Belfast: Ulsterman Publications, 1975.

Bog Poems. London: Rainbow Press, 1975. (With illustrations by Barrie Cooke.)

*North.** London: Faber, 1975. New York: Oxford University Press, 1976.

Robert Lowell: A Memorial Address and Elegy. London and Boston, Mass.: Faber, 1978.

Gravities. Newcastle: Charlotte Press, 1979. (With drawings by Noel Connor.)

*Field Work.** London and Boston, Mass.: Faber, 1979.

Selected Poems 1965–1975. London and Boston, Mass.: Faber, 1980.

Preoccupations: Selected Prose 1968–1978. London and Boston, Mass.: Faber, 1980.

Uncollected articles and reviews

'Out of London: Ulster's Troubles'. *New Statesman*, 1 July 1966, pp. 23–4.

'Old Derry's Walls'. *The Listener*, 24 October 1968, pp. 521–3.

'Celtic Fringe, Viking Fringe'. *The Listener*, 21 August 1969, pp. 254–5.

'Delirium of the Brave'. *The Listener*, 27 November 1969, pp. 757–9.

'King of the Dark'. *The Listener*, 5 February 1970, pp. 181–2.

'King Conchobor and his Knights'. *The Listener*, 26 March 1970, pp. 416–17.

'Views' (on living in Berkeley). *The Listener*, 31 December 1970, p. 903.

'Seamus Heaney Praises Lough Erne'. *The Listener*, 4 February 1971, pp. 142–3.

'A Poet's Childhood'. *The Listener*, 11 November 1971, pp. 660–1.

'Deep as England'. *Hibernia*, 1 December 1972, p. 13.

'Mother Ireland'. *The Listener*, 7 December 1972, p. 790.

'Lost Ulstermen'. *The Listener*, 26 April 1973, pp. 550–1.

'Land-Locked'. *Irish Press*, 1 June 1974, p. 6.

'Summoning Lazarus'. *The Listener*, 6 June 1974, pp. 741–2.

'John Bull's Other Island'. *The Listener*, 29 September 1977, pp. 397–9.

'Treely and Rurally'. *Quarto*, 9 (August 1980), p. 14.

'English and Irish'. *The Times Literary Supplement*, 24 October 1980, p. 1199.

'Osip and Nadezhda Mandelstam'. *London Review of Books*, 20 August–2 September 1981, pp. 3–6.

Poetry Book Society Bulletin, 61 (Summer 1969); 85 (Summer 1975); 102 (Autumn 1979).

Interviews

'Le Clivage traditionnel' (anon.). *Les Lettres nouvelles* (March 1973), pp. 187–9.

'Poets on Poetry' (Patrick Garland). *The Listener*, 8 November 1973, p. 629.

Interview (Harriet Cooke). *Irish Times*, 28 December 1973, p. 8.

'The Saturday Interview' (Caroline Walsh). *Irish Times*, 6 December 1975, p. 5.

'Unhappy and at Home' (Seamus Deane). *The Crane Bag*, 1, 1 (1977), pp. 61–7.

'An Interview with Seamus Heaney' (James Randall). *Ploughshares*, 5, 3 (1979), pp. 7–22.

'Brooding Images' (John Silverlight). *The Observer*, 11 November 1979, p. 37.

Interview. In Monie Begley, *Rambles in Ireland*, pp. 159–69. Old Greenwich, Conn.: Devin-Adair, 1977.

Interview. In John Haffenden, *Viewpoints: Poets in Conversation*, pp. 57–75. London: Faber, 1981.

SELECTED CRITICISM OF SEAMUS HEANEY

Books

Broadbridge, Edward (ed.). *Seamus Heaney*. Copenhagen: Danmarks Radio, 1977.

Buttel, Robert. *Seamus Heaney*. Lewisburg, Pa: Bucknell University Press, 1975.

Selected articles

Alvarez, A. 'A Fine Way with the Language'. *New York Review of Books*, 6 March 1980, pp. 16–17.

Anon. 'Fear in a Tinful of Bait'. *The Times Literary Supplement*, 17 July 1969, p. 770.

Anon. 'Semaphores of Hurt'. *The Times Literary Supplement*, 15 December 1972, p. 1524.

Bailey, Anthony. 'A Gift for Being in Touch'. *Quest* (January–February 1978), pp. 38–46, 92–3.

Bloom, Harold. 'The Voice of Kinship'. *The Times Literary Supplement*, 8 February 1980, pp. 137–8.

Brown, Terence. 'Four New Voices: Poets of the Present'. In *Northern Voices: Poets from Ulster*, pp. 171–213. Dublin: Gill and Macmillan, 1975.

Carson, Ciaran. 'Escaped from the Massacre?' *The Honest Ulsterman*, 50 (Winter 1975), pp. 183–6.

Curtis, Simon. 'Seamus Heaney's *North*'. *Critical Quarterly*, 18, 1 (Spring 1976), pp. 80–3.

Dunn, Douglas. 'Manana is Now'. *Encounter* (November 1975), pp. 76–81.

Ehrenpreis, Irvin. 'Digging In'. *New York Review of Books*, 8 October 1981, pp. 45–6.

Foster, John Wilson. 'The Poetry of Seamus Heaney'. *Critical Quarterly*, 16, 1 (Spring 1974), pp. 35–48.

Hederman, Mark Patrick. 'Seamus Heaney: The Reluctant Poet'. *The Crane Bag*, 3, 2 (1979), pp. 61–9.

Longley, Edna. 'Fire and Air'. *The Honest Ulsterman*, 50 (Winter 1975), pp. 179–83.

——'Stars and Horses, Pigs and Trees'. *The Crane Bag*, 3, 2 (1979), pp. 54–60.

——'Heaney: Poet as Critic'. *Fortnight* (December 1980), pp. 15–16.

Longley, Michael. 'Poetry'. In Michael Longley (ed.), *Causeway: The Arts in Ulster*, pp. 95–109. Belfast: Arts Council of Northern Ireland, 1971.

Mahon, Derek. 'Poetry in Northern Ireland'. *Twentieth Century Studies* (November 1970), pp. 89–93.

Miller, Karl. 'Opinion'. *The Review*, 27–8 (Autumn–Winter 1971–2), pp. 41–52.

McGuinness, Arthur E. 'The Craft of Diction: Revision in Seamus Heaney's Poems'. In Maurice Harmon (ed.), *Image and Illusion: Anglo-Irish Literature and its Contexts*, pp. 62–91. Portmarnock, Co. Dublin: Wolfhound Press, 1979.

O'Brien, Conor Cruise. 'A Slow North-East Wind'. *The Listener*, 25 September 1975, pp. 404–5.

Ricks, Christopher. 'Lasting Things'. *The Listener*, 26 June 1969, pp. 900–1.

——'The Mouth, the Meal and the Book'. *London Review of Books*, 8 November 1979, pp. 4–5.

Thwaite, Anthony. 'Neighbourly Murders'. *The Times Literary Supplement*, 1 August 1975, p. 866.

Waterman, Andrew. 'Ulsterectomy'. In Dannie Abse (ed.), *Best of the Poetry Year 6*, pp. 42–57. London: Robson, 1979.